BREAD FROM MY OVEN

By
MARJORIE PARKER

D0888229

MOODY PRESS
CHICAGO

ISBN: 0-8024-0910-5

Moody Press, a ministry of the Moody Bible Institute, is
designed for education, evangelization and edification.
If we may assist you in knowing more about Christ and
the Christian life, please write us without obligation to:
Moody Press, c/o MLM, Chicago, Illinois 60610.

29 30 28

Printed in the United States of America

BREAD UPON THE WATERS

ECCLESIASTES 11:1-6

If you are looking for a formula that will send forth the members of the family to their daily tasks with cheerful hearts prepared for discouragements, disappointments, or blighted hopes, then one may be found in the family altar.

Father and Mother will be stronger for the work ahead and determined to glorify God in whatever comes.

The family will be conscious throughout the day of the presence of the Holy Spirit so that they may be "more than conquerors" over all temptations that would ensnare them.

Home relationships and homelife will be sweetened. Misunderstandings will be resolved and frictions relieved, when the family prays together. Guests in the home will be blessed and friendships will be hallowed.

Best of all, it will be bread cast upon the waters which will give you 100 percent returns. Through family devotions, the eternal salvation of the children may be determined; and when the boys and girls have left the home, they will be held by the Christian ideal.

"Praying always with all prayer and supplication in the Spirit, and watching thereunto with all perseverance and supplication for all saints" (Eph 6:18).

A WISE WOMAN

PROVERBS 14:1

A good Christian home doesn't just happen. It is not the automatic result of seeing that the family is fed, clothed, and bathed daily. It is much more.

The wise woman (or the mother who cares) draws up some plans. She goes to the Bible daily for divine instruction in the building of her home. With Jesus Christ as the foundation, this house will stand against the storms of life.

"And, Thou, Lord, in the beginning hast laid the foundation of the earth; and the heavens are the works of thine hands" (Heb 1:10). Surely we can depend on the One who laid the foundation of the earth!

But this house must have walls—walls of prayer to keep Satan out, then "salvation will God appoint for walls and bulwarks" (Isa 26:1).

"Except the LORD build the house, they labour in vain that build it" (Ps 127:1).

> O God, our help in ages past,
> Our hope for years to come,
> Our shelter from the stormy blast,
> And our eternal home.
>
> ISAAC WATTS

HOUSE BEAUTIFUL

MATTHEW 6:19-21

All of us desire a lovely home with comfortable and attractive furnishings. Certainly our Lord would have us to be concerned with the comfort and welfare of the families He has entrusted to us.

But it is so easy to think more highly of these things than we ought to think. Our sense of values becomes somewhat upset when we put too great a value on things material.

Oliver Wendell Holmes said, "We sometimes mortgage a house for the mahogany we bring into it. Beauty is a great thing, but beauty of garment, house, and furniture are tawdry ornaments compared with domestic love. All the elegance in the world will not make a home, and I would give more for a spoonful of real hearty love than for whole shiploads of furniture and all the gorgeousness the world can gather."

What does God's Word say?

"Better is little with the fear of the LORD than great treasure and trouble therewith. Better is a dinner of herbs where love is, than a stalled ox and hatred therewith" (Pr 15:16-17).

"It is better to dwell in a corner of the housetop, than with a brawling woman in a wide house" (Pr 21:9).

> O think of the home over there,
> By the side of the river of light,
> Where the saints all immortal and fair
> Are robed in their garments of white.
>   D. W. C. HUNTINGTON

TO LOVE AND TO CHERISH

1 JOHN 4:7-12

"A feeling of strong personal attachment induced by sympathetic understanding" is the way Webster defines love. But we know love as that tender, considerate affection that we all need. It is the greatest of these three: faith, hope, and love.

Christians should walk in love. We should love God supremely, and our neighbor as ourselves. One indication that we have eternal life is that we love God and the brethren, for he that loves, has God and knows God.

Does your heart ever feel bereft of love? Benjamin Franklin said, "If you wish to be loved, be lovable."

Remember that love is a fruit of the Spirit and that love must be shed abroad in our hearts by the Holy Spirit. So if you want more love, you must be filled with the Spirit. If you are filled with God's love, you will become a channel and God will love others through your love.

"Be kindly affectioned one to another with brotherly love; in honor preferring one another" (Ro 12:10).

> Love lifted me! Love lifted me!
> When nothing else could help,
> Love lifted me.
>
> JAMES ROWE

THE TONGUE

EPHESIANS 4:29-32

Enjoyment and relaxation can come to the housewife by a friendly chat with a neighbor over a cup of coffee after the children have been hustled off to school. Or a pleasant conversation over the telephone can brighten one's day. On the other hand, much harm can be done to another's life and reputation if such an innocent pastime as mentioned here is turned into a gossip session.

The Bible deals more severely with the tongue than with any other member of the human body. For one person "corrupt communication" may be profanity; for another it may be subtle innuendo, and for another, gossip.

What can be done? Refrain from any speech except that which will edify or build up the hearers in the knowledge of whatsoever things are true, honest, just, pure, lovely, and of good report.

Napoleon said that we rule men with words. How carefully, then, these words ought to be chosen and weighed before being uttered.

"Let the words of my mouth, and the meditation of my heart, be acceptable in thy sight, O LORD, my strength, and my redeemer" (Ps 19:14).

> O for a thousand tongues to sing
> My great Redeemer's praise,
> The glories of my God and King,
> The triumphs of His grace.
>   CHARLES WESLEY

"NO THANKS"

Psalm 103:1-7

Isn't it strange that very often we forget to thank God for our blessings until it suddenly dawns on us that Thanksgiving Day is here, and that it is a day when we are supposed to give thanks for all of life's bounties.

Too often the real purpose of the day is obscured by the frenzy of getting the groceries in, the turkey cooked, the dressing made, the table set, the house cleaned, et cetera, ad infinitum!

A real comprehension of the truths which cluster about Thanksgiving can come only by a service of praise at church, or a quiet time spent alone with God and His Word.

It seems so much easier to be conscious of problems and cares which are about to overwhelm us, than it is to "Count your many blessings, name them one by one, and it will surprise you what the Lord has done."

But when we take inventory of all our blessings our problems and burdens seem to fade into insignificance.

"Giving thanks always for all things unto God and the Father in the name of our Lord Jesus Christ" (Eph 5:20).

> When morning gilds the skies,
> My heart awaking cries,
> May Jesus Christ be praised:
> Alike at work and prayer,
> To Jesus I repair;
> May Jesus Christ be praised.
>
> Trans. from the German by
> EDWARD CASWELL

NOT BY BREAD ALONE

DEUTERONOMY 8:1-3

Hippies today use the word bread to mean money, or cash. This would indicate that even in their thinking, bread is necessary to life, just as is the coin of the realm.

But the Word of God tells us that man does not live by bread alone—be it food *or* cash—"but by every word that proceedeth out of the mouth of the LORD."

It would follow then that man (or woman) would do well to take heed to "every word that proceedeth out of the mouth of the LORD."

Where may we find such words? Where can we go to find guidance for our daily walk? "Thy word have I hid in mine heart, that I might not sin against thee" (Ps 119:11).

There are many things that money (or "bread") *can* buy. But they are not the things that make for happiness. Money can help to make us more comfortable in this world—comfortable in our misery sometimes—but food for the soul comes from the Word of God and communion with Him. Feed on His Word. The nourishment is there for the taking.

> Ere you left your room this morning
> Did you think to pray?
> In the name of Christ, our Saviour,
> Did you sue for loving favor,
> As a shield today?
> MRS. M. A. KIDDER

9

SPEAKER OF THE HOUSE

EPHESIANS 5:22-33

There are many times and situations when the wife and mother is obliged to be the "speaker of the house."

Those mothers whose homes are broken, or whose husbands are in the service of their country, of necessity must act as head of the house.

In normal circumstances, however, this is not God's way. He does things decently and in order and anything with two heads is a monstrosity. So there must be only one head in every home. This is clearly stated in His Word, "For the husband is the head of the wife" (v. 23).

The wife who is submissive to her husband in love makes it easy for him to obey the scriptural injunction, "So ought men to love their wives as their own bodies" (v. 28).

Someone has said, "Some women cling to their own houses like the honeysuckle over the door, yet, like it, sweeten all the region with the subtle fragrance of their goodness."

> Saviour, teach me day by day,
> Love's sweet lesson to obey;
> Sweeter lesson cannot be,
> Loving Him who first loved me.
>
> JANE E. LEESON

BLESSINGS IN DISGUISE

MATTHEW 5:44-48

Two nurses came to a doctor saying they could not bear serving a certain patient who was most trying. The doctor pointed out to them that the patient was educating them, and such training was well worth paying for. He told them that if they could stand it they would reap the benefit throughout life; they would be tempered and nothing would be too hard for them again. They took up the work once more from a different point of view and never complained again.

In our humanity it is difficult to understand sometimes, but it is well to remember in times of trial that there is a bright side to all things and a good God over all.

Charles Haddon Spurgeon said, "Somewhere or other in the worst flood of trouble there always is a dry spot for contentment to get its foot on, and if there were not it would learn to swim."

"And we know that all things work together for good to them that love God, to them who are the called according to his purpose" (Ro 8:28).

> Just when I need Him, Jesus is near,
> Just when I falter, just when I fear;
> Ready to help me, ready to cheer,
> Just when I need Him most.
>
> WILLIAM C. POOLE

JOY BELLS

MATTHEW 6:1-4

Are you one of those rare people who can do a friend a favor on the sly? Or do you have to "sound a trumpet" when you do a good deed, so that all the world may know?

There is a special kind of satisfaction that comes from doing good and keeping it a secret. Those who practice this higher altruism know an inner joy experienced by very few indeed.

This type of Christian service will ring joy bells that have never been heard before, bringing joy to the recipient of the deed as well as joy to the doer.

Of course the secret joy spreader must cultivate this trait. It will not come naturally, because it goes against the grain of our ego. We want others to recognize any noble or unselfish act of ours.

Jesus was our wonderful example of doing good secretly. He warned against ostentatious charity and admonished His followers, "Take heed that ye do not your alms before men, to be seen of them" (Mt 6:1).

When He healed the leper He told him, "See that thou tell no man," and left the scene at once.

> Ring the bells of heaven! there is joy today,
> For a soul returning from the wild!
> See! the Father meets him out upon the way,
> Welcoming His weary, wand'ring child.
>
> WILLIAM O. CUSHING

TELL HIM YOU LOVE HIM

1 JOHN 4:15-21

Every wife knows that to speak the simple sentence, "I love you," will ease strained relations and restore fellowship in many domestic situations. Any husband is pleased to have his wife repeat these three little magic words.

Often a child's attitude can be changed from stubborn rebellion to submissive obedience by Mother's simply saying to him, "I love you," accompanied of course by a smile which tells him she really means it.

Who is not made happier by a sincere verbal expression of love?

So also, the loving heart of our God must be warmed when we tell Him that we love Him. He above all, through Christ Jesus, is worthy of the frequent expression of our love.

One look at a sunrise should cause us to exclaim, "I love thee, my Jesus."

One note of birdsong should prompt us to sing out, "I love thee, my Lord."

The heart's view of Calvary should inspire us to respond,

> My Jesus, I love Thee,
> I know Thou art mine;
> For Thee all the follies of sin I resign;
> My gracious Redeemer, my Saviour art Thou;
> If ever I loved Thee, my Jesus, 'tis now.
>
> W. R. FEATHERSTONE

WORDS OF WISDOM

PROVERBS 4:10-13

These strong words are appropriate for young sons and older sons, as well as daughters young and old.

All who are in Christ through faith in Him are the possessors of an all-sufficient Saviour, and have come to a knowledge which far exceeds all the knowledge and wisdom of the world, with all its progress in the arts and sciences.

To believe on Christ who is Wisdom from God is to possess real life, true liberty. Christ is wisdom indeed.

There are enough stumbling blocks and pitfalls in the paths of young people today. Surely they need all the help they can get so that when they run they will not stumble.

Blessed is the youngster—or teenager—who will "take fast hold of instruction; let her not go: keep her; for she is thy life" (v. 13).

God's instruction book will tell us the way if we will study it; for He says, "I am the way, the truth, and the life: no man cometh unto the Father, but by me" (Jn 14:6).

> Saviour, teach me day by day,
> Love's sweet lesson to obey;
> Sweeter lesson cannot be,
> Loving Him who first loved me.
>
> JANE E. LEESON

THE BREAD OF IDLENESS

PROVERBS 31:10-31

Many housewives today are complaining about being bored to death. Our government and others are spending billions of dollars to provide entertainment for our leisure hours. Labor unions are striking with demands for shorter workweeks and more leisure time for workers.

Why is it that some busy wives and mothers never find enough hours in the day to do the many tasks at hand, while others seem oblivious to their duties and spend the daytime hours chatting on the telephone or sipping a cup of coffee at the neighbor's?

Surely there is no harm, and sometimes much to be gained, by a friendly visit with a neighbor. But as in all things, the concerned housewife and mother will not allow these pleasantries to take too large a share of her time lest she be guilty of eating "the bread of idleness."

It is no secret that work has a therapeutic value and that one is happiest when busy. Working in the sunshine among the flowers has helped to heal many a broken heart.

Any woman who "looks well to the ways of her household" will have no time to become bored. Instead, "Strength and honour are her clothing; and she shall rejoice in time to come" (v. 25).

> The sweetest lives are those to duty wed,
>   Whose deeds, both great and small,
> Are close-knit strands of unbroken thread
>   Where love ennobles all.
> The world may sound no trumpets, ring no bells;
> The book of life the shining record tells.

> Attributed to
> ELIZABETH BARRETT BROWNING

15

SENIOR CITIZENS

PROVERBS 20:24-29

There comes a time for all of us when we must face the fact that the years are piling up and we are no longer young. The telltale wrinkles are a little deeper than the last time we looked.

So what? Someone has said, "If wrinkles must be written upon your brow, let them not be written upon the heart. The spirit should not grow old."

Old age is blessed if you let it come naturally. You cannot hide it. Oh, you may cover the wrinkles for a while, but not for long. If the time has come for you to be old do not be ashamed of it!

Did you ever stop to think that the grandest things in the universe are old—mountains, rivers, seas, stars, even eternity. Old age is glorious if found in the way of righteousness.

In describing the aged man, Solomon likens the whiteness of his locks to the blossoming of the almond tree. "A hoary head is a crown of glory." When one comes to the end of the path of life, there may be no color in the cheek, no luster in the eye, no spring in the step, yet around the head of the aged one who has been "faithful unto death" there may glow a glory brighter than ever bloomed in an almond tree.

> My latest sun is sinking fast,
> My race is nearly run;
> My strongest trials now are past
> My triumph is begun.
>
> J. HASCALL

WHAT'LL I WEAR?

MATTHEW 6:27-30

This is a dilemma faced by the average woman almost every day. And a question the average husband probably is tired of hearing. There can be a closet full of clothes, yet there doesn't seem to be just the right dress for the occasion!

"Clothes make the man" it is said, and some might argue with this, but at least clothes make the woman feel more comfortable. And she is more at ease when she knows she is appropriately dressed.

There is much we can learn from the flowers which wear such beautiful garments. "And why take ye thought for raiment? Consider the lilies of the field, how they grow; they toil not, neither do they spin: and yet I say unto you, That even Solomon in all his glory was not arrayed like one of these" (vs. 28, 29).

Flowers do not save their best clothes for Sunday, but wear their lovely raiment and give forth their perfume every day. So let our Christian lives, free from stain, give forth the fragrance of the love of God.

> O Jesus, I have promised
> To serve Thee to the end;
> Be Thou forever near me,
> My Master and my Friend;
> I shall not fear the battle
> If Thou art by my side,
> Nor wander from the pathway
> If Thou wilt be my Guide.
>
> JOHN E. BODE

STARS

DANIEL 12:3

Outer space has come in for a great deal of attention in our modern day. The sun and moon and stars are being rediscovered and we are looking at them as though seeing them for the first time.

The Bible has much to say about the stars. God knows how many there are, and He has given each one a name (Ps 147:4). And it was a particularly bright star that led the Magi on the road to Jerusalem two thousand years ago.

Modern day astronomers with their technological advances, their powerful telescopes and computers, have added much to our knowledge of these heavenly bodies. But no one has yet been able to count the stars! "Look now toward heaven, and tell the stars, if thou be able to number them." (Gen 15:5).

It may be that God gave us the stars in their beauty to cause us to look up—up and away from ourselves and our daily frustrations and fears to take a far look away from ourselves. Better still, let us look beyond the stars to God who made them!

"Is not God in the height of heaven? and behold the height of the stars, how high they are" (Job 22:12).

I am thinking today of that beautiful land
I shall reach when the sun goeth down;
When thro' wonderful grace by my Saviour I stand,
Will there be any stars in my crown?

ELIZA E. HEWITT

"THANK YOU"

PSALM 107:8, 9

A mature Christian is one who can say "Thank You" to God when her husband fails to get that long-hoped-for raise in salary; or Johnnie brings home an "F" on his report card; or the baby comes down with measles in spite of all precautions.

When troubles pile up around us we can easily forget that He knows the end from the beginning and that this thing is going to work out for our good, no matter how dark the picture looks at the present time.

We forget that one must suffer before he can be healed.

If our gratitude depends on outward circumstances, it does not occupy a permanent place in our lives. When the winds of adversity blow, and we are in trouble and need help and still can say to God "Thank You," we have gained spiritually.

Are you lonely? Are you hungry? "He satisfieth the longing soul, and filleth the hungry soul with goodness" (v. 9).

Have you ever said "Thank You" to God for the warmth of the sun, the fragrance of a flower, the love of a child?

> Thank you, Lord, for saving my soul.
> Thank you, Lord, for making me whole.
> Thank you, Lord, for giving to me
> Thy great salvation so rich and free.
>
> SETH SYKES

WORRY WART

ISAIAH 26:1-4

Worry! Fret! Stew! Satan is pleased when that is the order of the day for us.

Faith and worry cannot be reconciled. Worry is a great hindrance to spiritual progress. God does not will that His own should be irritable, embittered, robbed of sleep, and have the peace of home destroyed by worry.

All the promises in His Word are given as insurance against such. No child of God who believes sincerely that all things work together for his good could constantly worry.

The first time you evaluate a situation and realize that it is beyond you, commit it to God and stop worrying.

Satan would have you turn your mind into a merry-go-round. He is the instigator of worry which displeases our Lord.

If we are children of God, let us quit this bad business of worrying. Why worry when you can pray?

"Peace I leave with you, my peace I give unto you: not as the world giveth, give I unto you. Let not your heart be troubled, neither let it be afraid" (Jn 14:27).

> Have we trials and temptations?
> Is there trouble anywhere?
> We should never be discouraged,
> Take it to the Lord in prayer.
>
> JOSEPH SCRIVEN

THE BREAD OF GOD

JOHN 6:30-35

Jesus is indeed the Bread of Life. He is the bread of God. Bread is a term used for food in a general sense.

Bread is essential as food for the body. Just so, there can be no spiritual life without Jesus.

Bread satisfies hunger, and every soul without Christ is a hungry soul. Oh, poor hungry soul, come to Jesus! He is the Bread that satisfies.

Bread is good to the taste. Nearly everyone thinks that his mother's bread was the best ever baked. There is no odor so pleasing to the olfactory sense as that of bread baking. Even now, in memory we can smell the delicious scent being wafted through the house. This is one of the most pleasant memories of childhood.

Bread gives strength. Weak soul, feed upon Jesus. He will strengthen you. "I can do all things through Christ which strengtheneth me" (Phil 4:13).

Surely the "bread" that God provides is good. "Oh taste and see that the LORD is good."

> My hope is built on nothing less
> Than Jesus' blood and righteousness;
> I dare not trust the sweetest frame,
> But wholly lean on Jesus' name.
>   EDWARD MOTE

PATIENCE

LUKE 8:4-15

One commodity that busy mothers are short on is patience. Just when you feel you have all your ducks in a row calamity strikes the household and patience flies out the window.

All of us praise patience, but few practice it. When the bones are aching with weariness; when time is running out and there is much yet to be done, Mom can lose patience and become irritable and cross.

But "natural" feelings must not rule the Christian, or what is her Christianity worth?

Remembering our patient Saviour ought to make it easier for His children to be patient.

"Grin and bear it is the old fashioned advice, but sing and bear it is a great deal better." So said Charles Haddon Spurgeon.

"What can't be cured must be endured," is true.

When our hearts are right with God how wonderfully He gives much grace to bear even the heaviest yoke. Only those with God's love in their hearts can sing at labor while others murmur.

> Sing the wondrous love of Jesus,
> Sing His mercy and His grace;
> In the mansions bright and blessed,
> He'll prepare for us a place.
>
> ELIZA E. HEWITT

WHAT'S IN A NAME?

MATTHEW 1:21-23

Loving parents very carefully select just the right name for that precious, newborn baby. Many children are named for relatives who are dear to the parents. At any rate, much thought is usually given to the naming of a child.

Some of the men in Scripture were named by God to indicate their characters or a blessing from God. This is why Jacob had his name changed to Israel and why Simon had his name changed to Peter.

Likewise, the names of Christ show His person and work. They reveal what He is and what He came to do. All of them are significant, for they all have important meaning for us; they unveil His true character.

The name "Jesus" was given by the angel to Joseph before Christ was born. It literally means "Saviour." Christ came to save us from our sins and to give us fellowship with God Himself.

The name Emmanuel, which means, "God with us," emphasizes the constant presence of God.

"A good name is rather to be chosen than great riches, and loving favour rather than silver and gold" (Pr 22:1).

> Take the name of Jesus with you,
> Child of sorrow and of woe;
> It will joy and comfort give you,
> Take it, then, where'er you go.
> MRS. LYDIA BAXTER

NEW YEAR'S RESOLUTIONS

2 Corinthians 5:14-17

Resolutions may be made and broken year after year, but it never hurt anyone to keep on making them. Better to live up to them for even a little while than never make them at all! And stifling a good impulse is never wise.

Of course resolutions made in the energy of the flesh, and resolutions dependent on one's own strength for their fulfillment, are easily forgotten, broken, or neglected.

But it is a different story when one determines by the help of the Lord to strengthen a weak place, or spread a little more joy in a sad world, or show a lost one the way of salvation.

Every New Year holds golden opportunities which we often let slip through our hands. When the strength of the Lord is relied upon, definite progress in the spiritual life will be made.

Never hesitate to follow your good impulses in making resolutions, then trust God for the power to carry them out!

> Father, Thy mercies past we own,
>   Thy still continued care;
> To Thee presenting, through Thy Son,
>   Whate'er we have or are.
> Our residue of days or hours
>   Thine, wholly Thine, shall be;
> And all our consecrated powers
>   A sacrifice to Thee.
>
> Charles Wesley

REJOICE EVERMORE!

HABAKKUK 3:17-19

No one but a Christian can be truly happy and every Christian ought to be supremely happy. We do not have to wait until we get to heaven to be happy. Our eternal life begins as soon as we let Jesus come into our hearts.

This is not the type of joy which kicks up its heels or laughs raucously, but rather the deep-seated peace which comes from the knowledge that sins have been forgiven and "your body is the temple of the Holy Ghost which is in you, which ye have of God, and ye are not your own" (1 Corinthians 6:19).

This is a joy that is permanent and is not tied to circumstances.

The Christian will be "found unto praise and honour and glory at the appearing of Jesus Christ"; but Peter adds, "Whom having not seen, ye love; in whom, though now ye see Him not, yet believing, ye rejoice with joy unspeakable and full of glory" (1 Pe 1:7, 8).

This is a joy that comes as a by-product of the acceptance of God's great gift—the Lord Jesus Christ.

"Glory ye in his holy name: let the heart of them rejoice that seek the LORD" (1 Ch 16:10).

> Come, we that love the Lord,
> And let our joys be known;
> Join in a song with sweet accord,
> And thus surround the throne.
>
> ISAAC WATTS

WORK AND WORSHIP

PSALM 33:13-15

No one can ever earn his salvation. "For by grace are ye saved through faith; and that not of yourselves: it is the gift of God: Not of works, lest any man should boast" (Eph 2:8-9).

After one has received this wonderful gift, however, his desire should be to serve the Saviour. "For they that are after the flesh do mind the things of the flesh; but they that are after the Spirit the things of the Spirit" (Ro 8:5).

Work, worship, and instruction are always the ingredients of Christian living. True worship of Christ always leads to the place of need where work should be done. Then the busy Christian will constantly need to go to the Lord and His Word for instruction and admonition.

It does not matter where your work is, or whether it is visible. You may never see the results of your labor. Your name may never be associated with it. But you are working with eternity in view!

> Make use of me, my God!
> Let me not be forgot;
> A broken vessel cast aside,
> One whom Thou needest not.
> All things do serve Thee here,
> All creatures, great and small;
> Make use of me, of me, my God—
> The meanest of them all.
>
> HORATIUS BONAR

THE BREAD OF TEARS

PSALM 80:1-5

Never be ashamed of your tears. Maudlin, cry-baby sobs are unbecoming in an adult, but tears of compassion or sympathy reveal qualities of the soul that this old world greatly needs.

Eight times Joseph is said to have wept; David seven times; and Jeremiah, the weeping prophet, three times. The shortest verse in the Bible tells us that "Jesus wept" (Jn 11:35).

God sends occasions to all when the greatest and the best of us give way to "the bread of tears."

God does not despise our tears. David pleaded, "Put thou my tears into thy bottle; are they not in thy book?" (Ps 56: 8).

So to weep is not wrong, that is, if we weep over the right things.

There is the comforting promise in Isaiah 25:8, "He will swallow up death in victory, and the Lord God will wipe away tears from off all faces, and the rebuke of his people shall he take away from off all the earth: for the LORD hath spoken it."

> God shall "wipe away all tears;"
> There's no death, no pain, nor fears;
> And they count not time by years,
> For there is "no night there."
>
> JOHN R. CLEMENTS

DOERS OF THE WORD

JAMES 1:21-25

To hear is easier than to do. We hear the Word of God over and over and even rejoice in it, yet fail to let it take hold in our lives so that we act upon it.

If we are to be doers of the Word we must act out its principles in our daily living.

This involves many things: "bringing into captivity every thought to the obedience of Christ" (2 Co 10:5), walking "in wisdom toward them that are without, redeeming the time" (Col 4:5), and showing "forth the praises of Him who hath called you out of darkness into His marvelous light" (1 Pe 2:9).

In other words we must try to live moment by moment in the light of God's Word, "doing" according to the light it sheds upon our path.

We are clearly told that if we hear God's Word and do it not, we are deceiving ourselves.

One can look at his face in a mirror and quickly forget how he looked. So it is possible to see our spiritual image in the Word of God and forget how we appear.

God put His truths in His Book for our good. "Therefore we ought to give the more earnest heed to the things which we have heard, lest at any time we should let them slip" (Heb 2:1).

QUEEN FOR A DAY

PROVERBS 4:5-9

What fun it is to be granted a reprieve from housework for about twenty-four hours on your birthday or anniversary. The reprieve may take the form of breakfast in bed or dinner at a swank restaurant, and such luxurious treatment can produce a certain inner glow that will last for many days.

We read of a number of queens in the Bible. One was the famed Queen of Sheba who "came to Jerusalem with a very great train" to see with her own eyes if the stories of the splendor and majesty of Solomon's court were true. Convinced, before returning to her own country she said to Solomon, "The half was not told me: thy wisdom and prosperity exceedeth the fame which I heard" (1 Ki 10:7).

"Queen for a day" is about as long a reign as many of us will have here on earth. But what hope we have for the future! "If we suffer, we shall also reign with him" (2 Ti 2:12).

"The kingdoms of this world are become the kingdoms of our Lord, and of his Christ; and he shall reign for ever and ever" (Rev 11:15*b*).

> Jesus shall reign where'er the sun
> Does his successive journeys run;
> His kingdom spread from shore to shore,
> Till moons shall wax and wane no more.
>
> ISAAC WATTS

FROM RAGS TO RICHES

2 CORINTHIANS 8:7-9

Many stories have been told about some famous person who rose from rags to riches. We have thrilled to learn how a life begun in poverty triumphed by hard work and diligence and attained great wealth.

We would be more surprised, however, if we read of one of great wealth who gave up his riches to those who were poor and less fortunate and by so doing became poor himself.

Not many stories have been told of any who have gone from riches to rags in order that others might become rich. Yet that is exactly what our Lord did. He came from the glories of heaven, where all that the Father possessed He possessed, to live His earthly life in poverty. His poverty was voluntary. He *chose* to do this for your sake and my sake.

"The foxes have holes and the birds of the air have nests; but the Son of Man hath not where to lay His head" (Mt 8:20).

What was it that made Him do this for you and for me? "That ye through His poverty might be rich" (v. 9).

Down from His glory, ever living story,
My God and Savior came, and Jesus was His name.
Born in a manger, To His own a stranger,
A man of sorrows, tears and agony.
WILLIAM E. BOOTH-CLIBBORN

LET'S DEMONSTRATE!

MATTHEW 12:22-30

There are so many issues before us today that we are compelled to take a stand on one side or the other. All classes and types of people are carrying signs. We have protesters, demonstrators, marchers, and rioters.

Ours is a world of challenge, change, and conflict. Much time and money is spent in these interests today.

There is one issue we cannot dodge but must face squarely. We cannot be neutral: What will you do with Jesus?

If we do not line up on His side we are automatically against Him. Jesus said, "He that is not with me is against me" (v. 30). If you don't want to be *against* Him then you must march *for* Him.

Let's demonstrate! Let's show the world what Christ can do with a life wholly committed to Him. He can bring real meaning and direction into the life of one completely dedicated to Him.

> Take my life, and let it be
> Consecrated, Lord, to Thee;
> Take my hands, and let them move
> At the impulse of Thy love.
>   FRANCES R. HAVERGAL

A MORSEL OF BREAD

GENESIS 18:5   JUDGES 19:5   1 SAMUEL 28:22

We have many hungry people in the world today, and we Christian people should do all in our power to see that they are fed.

God does not intend for us to encourage laziness and indolence, and many times our efforts to help others who could help themselves result in this; however, God does expect us to help those who are less fortunate than we. We should count it a privilege to share our "morsel of bread," and thank God we have some to share. "It is more blessed to give than to receive."

To feel the pangs of hunger and have no bread is tragic. Even more tragic are "they which do hunger and thirst after righteousness" and cannot find spiritual food.

The privilege and responsibility of the believer is to share his spiritual "morsel of bread" with a neighbor or friend, who may not have the opportunity of hearing the Word of God proclaimed by a godly pastor who is interested in winning the lost.

> Is your life a channel of blessing?
> Is it daily telling for Him?
> Have you spoken the word of salvation
> To those who are dying in sin?
>
> H. G. SMYTH

DO YOUR OWN THING!

ISAIAH 43:19-21

Much talk has gone around lately among the so-called flower children about doing your own thing.

What is your particular "thing"? For the mother in the home it means being "all things to all men" for she is the hub of the wheel which keeps the home running.

The wife and mother cannot know what each day will hold for her and the loved ones in her household.

There will be new experiences, new challenges, new opportunities. There will be lessons to be learned, and undoubtedly new sorrows and heartaches.

But what is God's promise? "I will do a new thing"— more than we could ask or think. What do we want from God for our personal lives?

A greater knowledge of His Word?

A more effective prayer life?

More knowledge of Jesus Christ?

An opportunity to win a neighbor to Christ?

When we find ourselves out in the desert, and new wilderness experiences await us, what does He promise?

"I will give waters in the wilderness, and rivers in the desert to give drink to my people, my chosen" (v. 20).

SPARE THE ROD

Painful though it may be to spank that naughty but darling child, still it is a commandment in the Bible to parents. And both father and mother should stand together in this important matter. The future of the children depends upon it.

Discipline of the child, begun while he is very small, is most effective when done in love. "Chasten thy son while there is hope, and let not thy soul spare for his crying (Pr 19:18). We are not to spank just for the sake of spanking, but we are admonished to give instruction with the punishment.

"The rod *and reproof* give wisdom: but a child left to himself bringeth his mother to shame" (v. 15). Does this say also that mother should be sure she spends enough time with her child?

These are Bible orders which the conscientious Christian mother will carry out diligently, patiently, and prayerfully, being careful at the same time to set a good example. Then, we are promised, such consistent correction will be rewarded.

"Correct thy son, and he shall give thee rest; yea, he shall give delight to thy soul" (v. 17).

WHO'S WHO

JOHN 3:1-18

Not many of us will find ourselves listed in *Who's Who of American Women*. Biographies will be found there of outstanding American women who have made some contribution to the cultural or economic life of our country. But God has His own *Who's Who*. The Scriptures term it "The Book of Life." One need not earn a doctor's degree, or even a bachelor's degree, to be listed there. One does not have to be of any particular race or color to be included, nor be rich or poor.

But there is one definite requirement which must be met by all who would be named in this Book: "Ye must be born again" (Jn 3:7).

Do you qualify?

Nicodemus possessed many qualifications, for he was "a master of Israel." But he lacked the one thing that would qualify him to have his name written in the Lamb's Book of Life. He had not been born again!

> A ruler once came to Jesus by night,
> To ask Him the way of salvation and light;
> The Master made answer in words true and plain,
> "Ye must be born again."
>
> W. T. SLEEPER

FAITH WORKETH PATIENCE

JAMES 1:1-4

Faith, work, and patience operate together. They are not to be separated. Believers are to exercise faith and then work and wait. If your faith goes to work, patience will follow. "That ye be not slothful, but followers of them who through faith and patience inherit the promises" (Heb 6: 12).

In simple terms, faith works and patience waits. We see these three working together again in 1 Thessalonians 1:3: "Remembering without ceasing your work of faith, and labor of love, and patience of hope in our Lord Jesus Christ."

Do you have these three spiritual friends in your life?

Someone has said, "Most footprints in the sands of time are made by workshoes."

Faith will either remove mountains or tunnel through.

> My faith looks up to Thee,
> Thou Lamb of Calvary,
> Saviour divine!
> Now hear me while I pray,
> Take all my guilt away,
> O let me from this day
> Be wholly Thine!

> RAY PALMER

36

THAT GREEN-EYED MONSTER

JAMES 3:14-18

Envy will prevent us from getting the most out of life, if we let it. Most of us would be happier if we could lower our envy-jealousy quotient. We can make ourselves miserable by grieving over the fact that Mrs. Jones' clothes are so much smarter than ours.

So what? Accept it as a challenge and use it to see how smart *you* can look on the amount of money you have to spend. Make it a game and the results will probably surprise even you.

Does a neighbor's new mink or expensive car bring to the surface that green-eyed monster? Then stop and count your own blessings! Maybe it took something like this to make you see how much you really have to be thankful for.

A person who is fully aware of her own joys is not as likely to resent the joys of others. A sense of humor helps too. One who can laugh at her own shortcomings or misfortunes when her eyes start turning green, will undoubtedly be spared the pangs of envy.

There may always be someone who is richer, prettier, and smarter than you, but if the truth were known, that one probably envies you. You may have some talent that she doesn't possess.

There can be no peace of mind where "envying and strife is."

"And the fruit of righteousness is sown in peace of them that make peace" (v. 18).

THE BREAD OF WICKEDNESS

It is not necessary to eat the "bread of wickedness" to know how bitter it tastes. There are many dangers in this kind of "bread." It is best not to investigate but to pass by it altogether. We do not have to experiment with certain things to know whether they are evil. It is imperative that a child of God not allow himself to be ensnared by the devil.

The way of wickedness is just the opposite from the way of wisdom. We are advised to "enter not"; "go not in"; "avoid it"; "turn from it." Travelers on the way of wickedness have a food all their own. They eat the "bread of wickedness" and drink the "wine of violence."

As a normal person partakes of food and drink, so do these wicked ones indulge in certain sins just as regularly. Sin becomes a definite part of their existence. Gradually this "food" becomes a part of them as food does for the normal body.

The believer's cup runs over with joy. His main source of energy is the "meat of the Word."

"Thy words were found, and I did eat them; and thy word was unto me the joy and rejoicing of mine heart" (Jer 15: 16).

TURN ON THE LIGHT

PROVERBS 4:18-27

Did you ever stop at the close of a day to trace the guiding hand of God in your experiences of that day? Try it sometime!

One does not stand still in His Christian life. The closer one walks with Jesus the more light He will shed on the path. If we walk in the light on the path He chooses for us, we will find it "shineth more and more unto the perfect day." This light comes principally from His Word and this is why He tells us, "Attend to my words; incline thine ear unto my sayings."

We should never become careless about the Word of God. It should be used daily to guide our lives, then we will have the assurance that all our ways will be established. The way of light is the way of life. God's light will enable us to control lips, and eyes, and feet. We shall be led in a straight course unto the "perfect day." The light is there—turn it on!

> Lead, kindly Light, amid th' encircling gloom,
> Lead Thou me on:
> The night is dark and I am far from home;
> Lead Thou me on!
> Keep Thou my feet; I do not ask to see
> The distant scene; one step enough for me.
>
> JOHN H. NEWMAN

YESTERDAY, TODAY, AND TOMORROW

MATTHEW 6:30-34

Wouldn't you feel sorry for someone who never had burdens, trials, or tribulations? How could that one grow strong to meet the storms of life which inevitably come? Such a person might be likened to a marshmallow—too soft and too sweet. How does an oak tree grow strong? Bending in the wind day by day, it develops resistance against the storms that beat upon it.

Yesterday is gone forever. I cannot undo any act of mine or unsay any word. All I can do at this point is commit all to God and pray for grace to do better tomorrow. I must be concerned with today. With faith in God and trust in His promises I can fight the battles of today and bear its burdens. "As thy days, so shall thy strength be" (Deu 33:25).

We are admonished to live but one day at a time and leave the yesterdays and tomorrows in the hands of the God of love. So let us journey but one day at a time.

> "Day by day," the promise reads,
> Daily strength for daily needs:
> Cast foreboding fears away;
> Take the manna of today.
>
> Thou my daily task shalt give:
> Day by day to thee I live;
> So shall added years fulfill,
> Not my own, my Father's will.
>
> JOSIAH CONDER

ENDURE HARDNESS

2 TIMOTHY 1:6-9

So long as we determine to faithfully serve our Lord and bear witness to His saving grace, we may be sure we will incur the wrath of Satan.

Should we let this discourage us? Not at all! Warfare in a righteous cause can be most rewarding. "Fight the good fight of faith, lay hold on eternal life" (1 Ti 6:12). The way to get the most out of the Christian life is to stand boldly for the truth.

Paul wrote to Timothy, "Thou therefore endure hardness, as a good soldier of Jesus Christ" (2 Ti 2:3). He is a poor soldier indeed who cannot "take it." With the power of Christ working in us and through us, we can withstand the attacks of our adversary, the devil, and do a real work for God.

> Must I be carried to the skies
> On flowery beds of ease,
> While others fought to win the prize,
> And sailed through bloody seas?
> Sure I must fight if I would reign;
> Increase my courage, Lord;
> I'll bear the toil, endure the pain,
> Supported by thy word.
>
> ISAAC WATTS

DELIGHT IN DEVOTIONS

PSALM 5:1-3

How difficult it is in the early part of the day to sneak away from the family, the telephone, and the household duties, find a quiet place, and take in some food for the soul!

Have there been days when there was not even time for that piece of toast and cup of coffee in the early morning, and as the day wore on you found yourself becoming weak physically? Yet how foolish we are to think that our spiritual life can be nourished and grow strong without the necessary food for the soul, and that on a day-by-day, meal-by-meal basis. One can lean all day on a certain verse or passage of Scripture read during the early morning hours.

Much can be learned from the practice of George Müller, the man of faith who lived in nineteenth century England. In reciting the pattern of his devotions he said, "The first thing to be concerned about was not how much I might serve the Lord; but how I might get my soul into a happy state, and how my inner man might be nourished."

Devotions at the outset of the day can be a real delight. Meditate on the Word of God and obtain food for the soul. The seeking soul will find there all that is needed; and the believing and obedient heart will be made happy in the Lord.

"O God, thou art my God; early will I seek thee" (Ps 63:1).

ADVISE AND CONSENT

PROVERBS 14:1-6

"Mother, what should I do about—?" "Mother, may I go to—?" "Mother, is it all right if I—?"

If there is one thing Mom has to do all day long, it is "advise and consent." A thousand and one decisions, small and great, must be made daily in every household. Because Dad is at work, this task usually falls to Mom.

The homemaker at the beginning of each day would do well to pray as did Moses, "So teach us to number our days, that we may apply our hearts unto wisdom" (Ps 90:12). The concerned mother will not absent-mindedly say yes or no to requests for permissions from her offspring. But she will carefully weigh the effects of that permission granted in the light of what is best for her child.

As for advice, the Christian mother finds the Bible a guide book for the rearing of her children "in the nurture and admonition of the Lord." Within its pages may be found wise instructions for parents and children.

"Wisdom is the principal thing; therefore get wisdom: and with all thy getting get understanding" (Pr 4:7).

DAILY BREAD

At times, I have wished that I were a camel and could take in a great quantity of nourishment at one time and have it last for a long time. Like physical bread, spiritual bread should be consumed at intervals.

In an effort to slim down some curves we put ourselves on a rigid diet, yet we would not think of starving our bodies. Often, though, we put ourselves on a spiritual diet and starve our souls when we forget to take in our daily supply of bread from God's Word.

It may be an old cliché but it is nevertheless true that families that pray together stay together. God commanded the Israelites, "And these words, which I command thee this day, shall be in thine heart: and thou shalt teach them diligently unto thy children, and shalt talk of them when thou sittest in thine house, and when thou walkest by the way, and when thou liest down, and when thou risest up" (Deu 6:6, 7).

> We search the world for truth; we cull
> The good, the pure, the beautiful,
> From all old flower fields of the soul;
> And, weary seekers of the best,
> We come back laden from our quest,
> To find that all the sages said
> Is in the Book our mothers read.
> JOHN GREENLEAF WHITTIER: *Miriam*

ENTERTAIN STRANGERS

LUKE 14:12-14

Anything that is worthwhile takes work, and so does hospitality. There are so many things to think of—polishing the silver, setting the table, setting the house in order, scrubbing the children. But we are admonished to "Be not forgetful to entertain strangers." This does not mean that we are to go out into the highways and hedges and compel people we never laid eyes on to come in and have a cup of coffee! A time of relaxed social activity can help ease tensions as well as provide opportunities to witness to unsaved neighbors and friends.

Coffee and apple pie do not require a great deal of work, yet they can be a hub around which good Christian fellowship revolves. We find in the Bible many examples of gracious entertainment in the home. While some thought they were entertaining a stranger, they were actually host to an angel.

Love should motivate us to open our hearts and homes and show others that we care. Many spiritual values are to be gained not only for ourselves, but also for our families and our guests. "Be not forgetful to entertain strangers: for thereby some have entertained angels unawares" (Heb 13: 2).

THE GREATEST OF THESE IS LOVE

1 Corinthians 13

We hear much in today's world about love. Most of the songs about love sung by the modern rock groups are not about the kind of love mentioned in this chapter of God's Word. Most "love" emphasis today is not scriptural.

No love, it has been said, is as great as mother love. Scriptural love of a mother for her child is the kind which comforts when comfort is needed and chastens when chastening is needed.

"Charity (love) beareth all things . . . endureth all things." This sometimes means the mother punishes her child because she knows the child needs it, although it grieves her to have to do so, more than the punishment hurts the child. But she is comforted in her heart by the knowledge that her thoughts have been for the welfare and training of her child rather than for her own feelings.

What mother has not had to spank her child and then go off to her own room to cry after seeing her little one suffer under the chastening? She knows that for a time, at least, fellowship between them has been broken. So it must grieve the loving heart of God when He sees His children suffer for the sins they have brought upon themselves.

"He that loveth not knoweth not God; for God is love" (1 Jn 4:8).

> God pardons like a mother
> who kisses the offense
> into everlasting forgetfulness.
> Henry Ward Beecher

THINGS

MARK 8:34-38

For some it is a collection of cups and saucers, each with its particular story to tell. For others it is butterflies, or guns, or stamps, or an Indian-head coin collection. *Things.* Maybe it is an antique cupboard that belonged to Grandmother, or the gold watch that was Uncle John's. *Things.*

Nearly all of us have made a collection of something or other. And there is no particular harm in such an innocent hobby. But the danger comes in attaching too much importance to these *things.* Perhaps we give too much thought to them for "the morrow shall take thought for the *things* of itself." "They that are after the flesh do mind the things of the flesh; but they that are after the Spirit the things of the Spirit" (Ro 8:5).

How much better it is to store up "things of the Spirit." For we are admonished to "Take heed, and beware of covetousness: for a man's life consisteth not in the abundance of the things which he possesseth" (Lk 12:15).

> Take my silver and my gold,
> Not a mite would I withhold . . .
> Take my moments and my days,
> Let them flow in endless praise.
>
> FRANCES R. HAVERGAL

THOUGHTS ARE THINGS

PHILIPPIANS 4:8-9

The thoughts one entertains are the things one enjoys, and what one enjoys reveals what one is. If we entertain only those thoughts that are true, honest, just, pure, lovely, of good report, there will be little time for us to think of things which are evil. In other words, if we fill our minds with pure thoughts we crowd out those that are impure.

The words "think" and "thank" come from the same root. One who "thinks" right will want to "thank," because as a man "thinketh in his heart, so is he." As we think about our blessings our hearts will overflow with thanksgiving. One who is thankful to another will be thoughtful of that one—it works two ways.

> Now thank we all our God
> With heart and hand and voices,
> Who wondrous things hath done,
> In whom His world rejoices;
> Who, from our mother's arms,
> Hath blessed us on our way
> With countless gifts of love,
> And still is ours today.
>
> MARTIN RINKART
> Trans. by CATHERINE WINKWORTH

THORN IN THE FLESH

2 CORINTHIANS 12:9-11

"Why did this have to happen to me? What have I done to deserve this?"

There comes a time when we all ask these questions, feeling that a trial is undeserved and we are somehow being unjustly punished. These are times when God's promises scattered throughout His Word can be especially precious. His strength becomes greater in our weakness; His grace all-sufficient. When we turn it all over to Him, "the power of Christ" rests upon us.

Remembering that He knows the end from the beginning, our suffering is eased and the pain made bearable.

Paul was evidently tempted to believe that he could do a better work for His Lord if only that thorn in the flesh could be removed. God knew, in His infinite wisdom, that Paul would be a better man with the thorn.

Trials would be easier to bear if we could remember that by enduring something which we may regard as a hindrance or a handicap, we can bring more glory to God than if that undesired thing was removed. The glorious fact is that these do not have to be borne in our own feeble strength, but by His power in us!

"My grace is sufficient for thee: for my strength is made perfect in weakness" (v. 9).

THE MOUTH SPEAKETH

MATTHEW 12:34-37

Have you ever been seated in a restaurant next to a table of well-dressed men and found that their conversation, clearly audible at your table, was constantly punctuated with profanity? These same individuals would not dream of coughing in your face or sneezing into your food, yet they freely use foul language within your hearing range. Why do they do it?

Is it a mark of manliness? Does it indicate how clearly one's mind operates; or does it make his conversation more pleasing? One thing is clear—it is offensive to those of good breeding and Christian principle, and it is dishonoring to God who said. "Thou shalt not take the name of the LORD thy God in vain."

A famous writer tells us that in no other civilized nation is blasphemy part and parcel of the everyday speech of men, women, and even children, as it is in America. Profanity is a foul habit that degrades the user and dishonors a holy God. Let us teach our children to help eliminate this plague from our society.

"I will take heed to my ways, that I sin not with my tongue: I will keep my mouth with a bridle, while the wicked is before me" (Ps 39:1).

> Take my lips and let them be
> Filled with messages from Thee.
> FRANCES R. HAVERGAL

THE BREAD OF AFFLICTION

DEUTERONOMY 16:3   2 CHRONICLES 18:26

There are few of us who have not at one time or another eaten "the bread of affliction." Mature in Christ though we may be, in our humanity and weakness some of the afflictions our loving Lord sends into our lives are hard to bear. Does this mean God does not love us or has turned His back on us? On the contrary, "Whom the Lord loveth He chasteneth." Because the mother punishes her child for wrongdoing means she does love that child.

So God would be unjust to His children if He did not bring us back onto the straight path when we had strayed into sin. Many Christians will testify that God's chastening brought them into closer fellowship with Him, and when it was all over, they praised Him for sending it. Have you ever thanked God for your afflictions? Certainly this goes against the grain. But are we wholly consecrated to Him if we rebel against what He sends?

"Who shall separate us from the love of Christ? shall tribulation, or distress, or persecution, or famine, or nakedness, or peril, or sword? As it is written, For thy sake we are killed all the day long; we are accounted as sheep for the slaughter. Nay, in all these things we are more than conquerors through him that loved us" (Ro 8:35-37).

OBEDIENCE

1 SAMUEL 15:21-23

What mother's heart is not warmed when her child timidly approaches, holding out an awkwardly wrapped gift, purchased with a few pennies saved from an allowance. The act speaks words that the child is not able to utter, and the mother's heart responds in love. But dearer to the mother's heart than this beautiful gesture is an obedient child, one who shows his love by obedience for "to obey is better than sacrifice, and to hearken than the fat of rams."

An outward effort to obedience is not enough; a child must obey in his heart if he is to please his mother. So must God's child obey in his heart as well as in his actions, if he is to please God.

The Lord Jesus set the standard of heart attitude above mere outward practice for He declared, "This people draweth nigh unto me with their mouth, and honoureth me with their lips; but their heart is far from me" (Mt 15:8).

This, then, must be the case. The desire in the heart to obey should prompt the outward act of obedience. The child who loves his mother in his heart has little difficulty in obeying her.

In this day of grace, the commandments must still be kept in the heart, and there must be love and esteem if the commandments are to be obeyed.

> We'll bring the little duties
> We have to do each day;
> We'll try our best to please Him,
> At home, at school, at play:
> And better are these treasures
> To offer to our King,
> Than richest gifts without them;
> Yet these a child may bring.

The Book of Praise for Children, 1881

52

PEACE

In the symbols painted on walls or worn on necklaces, in the voices of young people carrying picket signs, we receive one main message these days: peace now. It is rather strange to notice that often those who demonstrate so loudly for peace, end up using violence themselves. "They speak not peace: but they devise deceitful matters against them that are quiet in the land" (Ps 35:20). There is a peace, however, that is available to all for the asking—peace with God through our Lord Jesus Christ. This peace cannot be found at any peace table, summit meeting, by winning a war, or signing a treaty.

The world gives peace as a doctor gives an anesthetic; Christ gives peace that is life, and hope, and strength. Christ gives heart peace. The peace of the world operates only in favorable circumstances. The peace of Christ is effectual in any circumstance.

By confident reliance upon the Lord, the believer may enjoy the peace of God in the midst of the alarming and disturbing circumstances of life. A heart and mind at rest amid the storms of life, guarded by the peace of God—this is real peace.

"Peace I leave with you, my peace I give unto you: not as the world giveth, give I unto you" (Jn 14:27).

HAPPY NEW YEAR

DEUTERONOMY 11:11-12

On January 1, we stand upon the verge of an unknown year. There lie before us 365 new days, and we should march toward them with confidence. None can tell what we shall encounter, what changes will come, or what new experiences await. The housewife delights in crisp new curtains for her clean windows; a fresh coat of paint on a soiled wall; a new piece of furniture in a vacant spot. Housekeeping chores take on a new dimension and seem to lose some of their drudgery.

But there are other areas in our lives where many of us would like to have a fresh start. L. F. Tarkington has written a poem called, "The Land of Beginning Again," which comes to mind at the beginning of each new year. We would all like to take a trip to that magic land, and we do every New Year.

Backed by God's Word, we have the comforting and cheering message that if we commit our days to Him one by one, He will be with us "from the beginning of the year even unto the end of the year" (v. 12).

> Behold, another year begins!
>   Set out afresh for heaven;
> Seek pardon for thy former sins,
>   In Christ so freely given.
> Devoutly yield thyself to God,
>   And on His grace depend;
> With zeal pursue the heavenly road,
>   Nor doubt a happy end.
>   SIMON BROWNE

ARE YOU LONELY?

JOSHUA 1:5-9

Do you feel that your life's work is done now that you have reared your children and they have gone from home? Do the hours of your day seem endless? Loneliness has led many an otherwise healthy person to the doctor's office or to the psychiatrist's couch. And older people are not the only lonely people in the world. Many children are lonely because their parents have too little time for them. Teenagers are often lonely because they feel misunderstood. Some married couples are lonely because work separates them.

It should be comforting to know that there are times when we need to be alone, to strengthen our inner stability and restore serenity for busier days. The psalmist tells us, "He leadeth me beside the still waters. He restoreth my soul" (Ps 23:2-3).

Why not put to good use these free hours (which you never had before) in service for the Lord? Surely there are many less fortunate souls who would be cheered by a visit, a newsy letter, or a friendly telephone call.

> It was alone the Saviour prayed in dark Gethsemane;
> Alone He drained the bitter cup and suffered there for me.
>
> BEN H. PRICE

MOTHER AS TEACHER

MARK 6:32-34

To her children, mother has to be a doctor, lawyer, teacher, preacher. One of the greatest privileges she has though is to be able to teach them certain Christian principles which can only be learned in the home. Her personal faith, peerless manners, and subtle wisdom in her relationships with others, is the birthright of her children.

Jesus as the perfect teacher possessed more qualifications of a good teacher than just a thorough knowledge of the subject matter. He was "moved with compassion," which is a necessary ingredient for becoming a good teacher. A love for the one being taught is essential in good teaching.

No one was ever more patient nor as kind as the Saviour. If Mother's teaching is to be effective she must cultivate these characteristics of the Saviour.

> An angel paused in his downward flight
> With a seed of truth and love and light;
> And he said, "Where must this seed be sown
> To bring most fruit when it is grown?"
> The Master heard what he said and smiled,
> "Go plant it for Me in the heart of a child."
>
> SELECTED

HIS SEED BEGGING BREAD

PSALM 37:18-28

God does not forsake His people. Not only does David say, I have "not seen the righteous forsaken, nor his seed begging bread" (v. 25), but this is reiterated in verse 28: "The LORD . . . forsaketh not His saints."

God's way is to reward righteousness and to punish sin. "Say ye to the righteous, that it shall be well with him . . . Woe unto the wicked! it shall be ill with him" (Is 3:10-11). Our only possibility of righteousness is through Christ.

The child of God is "His seed" but one who begs bread is someone who is in abject need with no resource. The two pictures do not fit together because the child of God, through Christ, has available to him all the resources of his heavenly Father.

Many troubled hearts have leaned upon His promise, "I will never leave thee, nor forsake thee" (Heb 13:5).

> My Father is rich in houses and lands,
> He holdeth the wealth of the world in His hands!
> Of rubies and diamonds, of silver and gold,
> His coffers are full; He has riches untold.
> I'm the child of a King, the child of a King!
> With Jesus, my Savior, I'm the child of a King!
>
> HATTIE E. BUELL

WITH THANKSGIVING

PSALM 95

The foundation of all prayer should be laid with thanksgiving. God desires that we be mindful of present blessings and past petitions granted, when we come before Him invoking divine favor. It could be that before we begin the asking, our loving God would have us stop and count our present blessings.

Every day ought to be a Thanksgiving Day for the child of God. Strange it is that we do not ordinarily recognize the common mercies of life. We have to see a blind man led by his dog, before we realize what a wonderful thing it is to be able to see. We have to see one who is lame before we are thankful for two good feet. A shame it is that we are so dull it takes the misfortunes of others to rouse us to acknowledge our own blessings.

"Who can tell how much a bird means by its song? The aroma of the flowers smells like incense, and the mist arising from the river looks like the smoke of a morning sacrifice. Oh, that we were as responsive!" said T. DeWitt Talmage.

How often do we thank God for the cool, sweet water we drink; the pure fresh air we breathe; the ability to hear someone say, "I love you?"

"O give thanks unto the LORD; for he is good: for his mercy endureth for ever" (Ps 106:1).

THINE OWN UNDERSTANDING

PROVERBS 3:1-6

To lean upon one's own understanding is to trust a frail and insecure support. This is to form and execute one's own plans in an independent spirit of self-confidence and self-reliance. Now these qualities can be good, when supported by the power of God. When we proceed without Him, we are living as if there were no God. One does not need a God if he can work out his own destiny. What folly!

As a child leans upon the wisdom, strength, and care of his parents, to trust in the Lord is to put full confidence in Him—to fully rely upon Him. This means one's entire commitment to the grace and truth of God with the abandonment of every attempt to save oneself by one's own strength or wisdom. God waits to care for, provide for, and sustain His own. The secret is to submit your will to His holy will. Then "He shall direct thy path."

Knowing all things, He knows what is best for His own and leads wisely and safely.

God never deceives; but man is deceived whenever he puts too much trust in himself. Man proposes, but God disposes.

THOMAS A KEMPIS

A GOOD NAME

Most of us go to great lengths to protect our good name. The wise Solomon said, "A good name is rather to be chosen than great riches" (Pr 22:1). We who know Him bear the name of the Lord Jesus. The impression unsaved men have of our Saviour and His salvation, is made from what they see in our lives. "Ye are our epistle written in our hearts, known and read of all men: . . . written not with ink, but with the Spirit of the living God; not in tables of stone, but in fleshy tables of the heart" (2 Co 3:2-3).

James writes in his epistle that the ungodly rich "blaspheme that worthy name by the which ye are called" (Ja 2:7) referring to that beautiful name of our Lord Jesus Christ; the name "which is above every name," the name in which alone we have salvation.

"Neither is there salvation in any other: for there is none other name under heaven given among men, whereby we must be saved" (Acts 4:12). Let us bear His name worthily!

> The name of Jesus is so sweet,
> I love its music to repeat;
> It makes my joys full and complete,
> The precious name of Jesus.
> I love the name of Him whose heart
> Knows all my griefs, and bears a part;
> Who bids all anxious fears depart—
> I love the name of Jesus.
>
> W. C. MARTIN

THE QUIET TIME

ISAIAH 40:28-31

Who more than today's busy mother needs to "run, and not be weary," to "walk and not faint"? For the Christian wife and mother this is essential. Prayer and the reading of God's Word are her lifeline to strength and wisdom for the untrodden path of the hours ahead. In this way she can have the assurance of His presence by her side and feel strengthened spiritually to meet the problems of the day.

Something will have to give if opportunity is to be found for this quiet time with God. Nothing should be allowed to interfere with it. There will be days when you will have to fight to preserve it. But what is any more important? The entire family will benefit from your inner strength and you can impart to them something from the loving source. Can you remember a day, however smooth the sailing, when you did not need a measure of strength, courage, wisdom, and guidance? You will find it right there in God's Word!

"Open thou mine eyes, that I may behold wondrous things out of thy law" (Ps 119:18).

> Thou callest me to seek Thy face,
> 'Tis all I wish to seek;
> To attend the whispers of Thy grace,
> And hear Thee only speak.
> With Thee conversing, we forget
> All time, and toil, and care;
> Labor is rest, and pain is sweet,
> If Thou, my God, art here.
>
> CHARLES WESLEY

A LIFT FOR YOUR LIFE

PSALM 5:1-3

We would be wise to begin the day with a prayer to God. It will sweeten and gladden us from the start. We are exhorted to "die daily," and it is best to die to self and sin early each morning.

Direct a prayer to God, a prayer of thanks for the rest of another night and the light of another day; a prayer of thanks for the opportunities and privileges, the joys and the blessings that come with each new day; a prayer of supplication asking for strength to meet and fulfill the responsibilities that press so heavily upon every child of God.

Ask for wisdom to solve the many problems that crowd into every day. Ask for power and perception to deal with others, and for a filling of the Holy Spirit in order to do His will. Pray and look up. Look up for the smile of His approval. Behold His handiwork in the heavens, and listen for His voice. Look up and be assured that God is there. "In the morning will I direct my prayer unto thee, and will look up" (v. 3).

"I will lift up mine eyes unto the hills, from whence cometh my help. My help cometh from the LORD, which made heaven and earth" (Ps 121:1-2).

THE BREAD OF ADVERSITY

ISAIAH 30:18-21

Someone has said, "It is not what happens to you, but the way you take it that counts." Can you "take it"? Life can be managed when all goes well, but what do we do when adversity strikes? Then and only then do we show our true colors. How easy it is to think that every other person's burden is light while our own is heavy. Too often it is our fancy rather than our fate.

When the "bread of adveristy" must be eaten, it does only harm to "kick against the pricks" and hurt the feet. As a tree bows in the wind, so must we in the face of adversity. Grumbling is a bad habit for the child of God, and when we complain we miss a blessing. The rainbow will follow the rain as surely as God is on His throne. Every night breaks into morning.

> Let sorrow do its work,
>   Send grief or pain;
> Sweet are Thy messengers,
>   Sweet their refrain,
> When they can sing with me,
> More love, O Christ, to Thee,
>   More love to Thee!
>   ELIZABETH P. PRENTISS

WELCOME, STRANGER!

DEUTERONOMY 10:18, 19

"I'm so glad to welcome you to our church this morning. We do hope you will come again." Simple sentences but they mean so much.

Have you ever visited in a church away from home and felt hurt because you were not greeted and made welcome by members of the congregation? Certainly we should go to church to worship God and sit under the teaching of the Word of God, but we will all confess to a feeling of warmth, when we are made welcome by God's people and sense an atmosphere of friendliness when visiting a new church. Where the Word of God is preached in the power of the Holy Spirit by the pastor, and received and worked out in the lives of the members of that church, there will be warmth and loving fellowship.

Before we were "in Christ" Paul tells us, "ye were strangers" but "now ye are *no more* strangers and foreigners, but fellow citizens with the saints, and of the household of God."

Visitors come into your church almost every Sunday. It is your privilege to help them become "no more strangers" to the grace and salvation of Jesus Christ, our Lord.

> He prayeth best who loveth best
> All things both great and small;
> For the dear God who loveth us,
> He made and loveth all.
>
> COLERIDGE

KING TUT

Luke 14:25-33

It is sad to note how ancient rulers, longing for immortality, spent a lifetime in futile effort to prepare for life after death.

In Cairo's Egyptian museum may be found evidences of King Tutankhamen's preparation for the afterlife. Two life-size, black wooden statues of this Pharaoh once stood guard over a sealed door leading into the burial chamber. There are two massive solid coffins and four immense wooden funerary chambers completely overlaid with gold leaf. King Tut's tomb also contains furniture inlaid with gold and semi-precious jewels, an exquisite throne chair, and a multitude of precious art objects of alabaster and gold, priceless and intricately fashioned jeweled ornaments. All these treasures were assembled to give Tutankhamen a secure place in eternity. He spent the wealth of his kingdom for a corner on eternal life.

How tragic when men try to gain eternal life by their own methods!

Jesus said, "My sheep hear my voice, and I know them, and they follow me: And I give unto them eternal life; and they shall never perish, neither shall any man pluck them out of my hand" (Jn 10:27-28).

"But what can mortal man do to secure his own salvation?" Mortal man can do just what God bids him do. He can repent and believe. He can arise and follow Christ as Matthew did.

WASHINGTON GLADDEN

A LITTLE KNOWLEDGE

2 PETER 1:1-9

Probably the reason a little knowledge is a dangerous thing is that "knowledge puffeth up." One gains a little knowledge and it puffs him up until he is convinced he has a lot of knowledge. It is necessary to begin with a little knowledge, and if that knowledge is "of God, and of Jesus our Lord," then "grace and peace (will) be multiplied unto you."

But we are to grow in the knowledge of our Lord and His Word because if we do not grow, we will backslide, and this is dangerous! God has left us His written Word for our instruction, and He has given us the Holy Spirit as our teacher. What more could one ask? Ah, but there are many adversaries—procrastination, laziness, other interests, etc., all bent on defeating us.

In His infinite knowledge of *us*. He has given this instruction: "Ye therefore, beloved, seeing ye know these things before, beware lest ye also, being led away with the error of the wicked, fall from your own stedfastness. But grow in grace, and in the knowledge of our Lord and Saviour Jesus Christ. To him be glory both now and for ever" (2 Pe 3:17-18).

WAIT ON THE LORD

JAMES 5:1-8

In the spring, homemakers are very enthusiastic about beautifying their yards. We rake, and dig, and plant, and almost daily run out to see if the seeds are coming up. If impatience gets the best of us however, and we rake away the earth to see if the seeds are germinating, the chances are we have ruined the plants. The winter frost must mellow the seed lying in the bosom of the earth, and the rains of spring must swell it, while the suns of summer mature it.

So it is with the Christian. The proper exercise of patience is one of the difficulties of the spiritual life. If we do not see some immediate results of our feeble efforts for the Lord, we are disappointed. For the soldier, marching is much easier than standing still. And while it may seem an easy thing to wait on the Lord, it is one of the things a Christian soldier must learn to do, even if it takes years of training.

"There may have been long delays in the fulfillment of promises; but delays are not denials, and it is better to let the fruit ripen before you pluck it," said Dr. F. B. Meyer.

"Rest in the LORD, and wait patiently for him: fret not thyself because of him who prospereth in his way, because of the man who bringeth wicked devices to pass" (Ps 37:7).

BREAD FROM HEAVEN

NEHEMIAH 9:7-15   JOHN 6:31

There are many hungry-hearted people in the world today. But can not the same God who sent bread from heaven in Old Testament days, feed His people in the twentieth century? "Blessed are they which do hunger and thirst after righteousness: for they shall be filled" (Mt 5:6).

Many are hungering and thirsting after righteousness. They are seeking but not finding. Some are not finding because they are looking in the wrong place. Some are not seeking in earnest. Others are finding a scant quantity but not enough to satisfy; they are getting all sorts of bread, but it is not the bread that is come down from heaven. Instead they are getting a kind of watered-down religion, and this is the worst kind.

Hungry-hearted one, you do not have to go hungry! He is the Bread of Life. Feed on Him! He satisfies every need.

> Bread of heav'n,
> On Thee we feed;
> For Thy flesh is meat indeed:
> Ever let our souls be fed
> With this true and living Bread.
>   JOSIAH CONDER

ARE YOU SAFE?

PROVERBS 29:25

The great cathedral of St. Paul stands in the center of London.

Once when passing by it, a number of people could be seen in the street with their eyes directed toward something high up on the steeple. There, almost out of sight, a man was working in a kind of cradle. He appeared to be in the utmost danger, but in fact was quite safe. A strong rope tied round him was fastened to a stout beam. The wind might blow around him, but he felt no alarm; he was safe.

Is this not a picture of the Christian? In the hour of his greatest weakness he looks up to heaven. There, seated on His eternal throne, is his Father. The Christian knows he is safe.

> Safe in the arms of Jesus,
> Safe on His gentle breast—
> There by His love o'er-shaded,
> Sweetly my soul shall rest.
> Hark 'tis the voice of angels,
> Borne in a song to me,
> Over the fields of glory,
> Over the Jasper sea.
>
> FANNY J. CROSBY

LITTLE CHILDREN

MATTHEW 18:1-6

Birth, the primary miracle of the world, brings the timeless delight of seeing a mother with her infant child. To be sure, there are times when she says she would sell him for half-price, but if you will notice, she is all the while kissing his button nose or fluffing that wisp of baby hair!

It was undoubtedly a mother who made a verb out of the noun "diaper" for it is she who has the loving responsibility to feed, to carry about, and to diaper him. But there is more to making a man or woman out of a baby than just holding, feeding, loving, or putting him down to sleep. Mother has to see the end from the beginning. She must know that the kind of training he receives in infancy will largely determine the kind of man he will be. "Even a child is known by his doings, whether his work be pure, and whether it be right" (Pr 20:11).

It is Mother who must see that seeds of the Word are sown from earliest childhood. Timothy was taught the scriptures as a child by his mother Eunice and his grandmother Lois.

Blessed is such a mother for she can say, "I have no greater joy than to hear that my children walk in truth" (3 Jn 4).

VIOLETS OR ZINNIAS

ISAIAH 40:1-8

Roses around the door can brighten any home, whether it be a cottage or a mansion. Someone who lives within has added a touch of beauty to a sometimes sad and sordid world. Jesus was a lover of beauty in nature, for He spoke of how the lilies grew; of fields white unto the harvest; of birds of the air. Indeed He is the Creator of all things beautiful.

The petals of a rose are soft to the touch, but they must be handled carefully or they will bruise. Azaleas with their delicate colors are beautiful to see, but they will produce only if soil and sunshine are exactly to their liking. Gladioluses will stand straight and tall, but if you bend them they will break. We admire the velvet of the violets, but they must constantly be encouraged. The morning-glory will bloom brightly in the morning but wilts in the heat of the day.

There are hardy varieties of flowers, however, that are the delight of the amateur gardener, for they do not need any special attention. The common zinnia and the vivid petunia seem willing to go on blooming day after day without having someone fuss over and pamper them. They keep on producing without expecting any special care.

There are all kinds of flowers and there are all kinds of Christians. What kind are you—a violet or a zinnia?

MIND YOUR OWN BUSINESS

1 Thessalonians 4:7-12

Paul clearly told his brethren in this passage, "Mind your own business." Some are not quiet because they do not take time to study. Some do not study because they are not quiet long enough. In our mad daily rush, how we need to take time out to meditate. Think! Pray! Study! Be often quiet! Listen to God! We can't hear Him speak to us because we will not be still.

"He leadeth me beside the still waters" (Ps 23:2). We who are Christ's should manifest a Christian spirit by minding our own business. This means we are not to mind the other person's business. It also means that we are to tend to our business.

A Christian, above all people, should be diligent in business. A Christian should work. Laziness is natural to most of us, but nature should not be the rule of a child of God. It is as sinful to yield to a natural tendency to do nothing as it is to yield to a natural tendency to commit overt sins.

There are times when we must rest, study, be quiet. Don't mind someone's else's business, but be sure you do mind your own. This can be done by the grace of God and must be done if we are to heed the injunction, "Study to shew thyself approved unto God, a workman that needeth not to be ashamed, rightly dividing the word of truth" (2 Ti 2:15).

HOME, SWEET HOME

JOHN 14:1-6

Home means different things to different people. To many of us, it means simple things—a crackling fire upon the grate, a shining teapot, or the warm smell of bread baking in the oven. But a real home will be more than these dear things we can see and feel and smell. It will be a friendly haven from the cares of the world, a retreat where the soul can rest, and the dwelling place of those who love you best. Loving hands will perform menial chores for love resides here; dusting, sweeping, and cleaning becomes a sacred rite. While it is true that "Stone walls do not a prison make," it is equally true that marble floors and gilded walls do not make a home.

There is a home, our heavenly home, which becomes dearer with each passing year. In that home, as believers, we shall meet again those who shared our earthly home and have gone on before.

There are many mansions in our Father's house, and Jesus has gone to prepare a place for His own.

> I've wandered far away from God,
> Now I'm coming home;
> The paths of sin too long I've trod,
> Lord, I'm coming home.
>
> WILLIAM J. KIRKPATRICK

THE BREAD OF SORROWS

PROVERBS 15:9-15

Someone remarked that your children step on your feet when they are little and step on your heart when they grow up. We know that those who are closest to us have the power to hurt us most, or to make us the happiest.

A good question is asked in Ezekiel 22:14. "Can thine heart endure, or can thine hands be strong, in the days that I shall deal with thee?"

God never sends to His children more than they can bear. No apothecary weighs the medicine for a patient with half so much exactness and care as God weighs out to us our trials—not one grain too much does He permit to be put on the scale. Job said, "Let me be weighed in an even balance" (Job 31:6). We usually are able to endure the present hour. "As thy days, so shall thy strength be" (Deu 33:25).

A loving and wise God does not gather the trials of many years into one. He knows this would overwhelm us. He sends first one, then another, removes both sometimes and may send a third, heavier, perhaps than either. But all is measured wisely to our strength, and the reed may be bruised but not broken.

> "Man of Sorrows," what a name
> For the Son of God who came
> Ruined sinners to reclaim!
> Hallelujah! What a Saviour!
>
> P. P. BLISS

74

FAMILY AFFAIR

Ephesians 3:13-21

God must love the family, for next to marriage, it is mankind's oldest institution, ordained of Him. He desires that we be in His family, and He yearns to be our Father. "God setteth the solitary in families" (Ps 68:6). He remembers the lonely one, that one whose heart is bereft of all human ties. He offers an invitation to accept His only begotten Son and be forever at home in God's family. To be "born again" into the family of God should be a family affair. The invitation is extended to parents and children alike.

Maybe God made families so sons and daughters could understand the love and protection of a heavenly Father. Maybe He made families so Mom and Dad could better understand His concern for His children. "That our sons may be as plants grown up in their youth; that our daughters may be as corner stones, polished after the similitude of a palace" (Ps 144:12).

To all of us, whatever our position in the family, He says, "Be ye therefore followers of God, as dear children; And walk in love, as Christ also hath loved us, and hath given himself for us an offering and sacrifice to God for a sweetsmelling savour" (Eph 5:1-2).

MOSES AND THE BULRUSHES

EXODUS 2:1-10

Riding down the Nile River today, one has the feeling of floating in biblical history. Long ago the ships of Crete and Phoenicia, when those lands were in the heyday of their power, sought its commerce and wealth. Some recall Cleopatra, the proud queen of Egypt, who fascinated Julius Caesar and Mark Anthony. For believers the Nile River brings to mind Moses, who first looked upon those waters from his floating cradle and lived beside those broad waters for the first forty years of his life.

The heart of every mother is warmed when she reads to her child the story of the baby Moses and the bulrushes. She can understand the feelings of the mother, who desperate to save the life of her son, wove him a cradle of bulrushes and hid him among the reeds at the river's brink. Every Sunday school child is thrilled by the story of the baby Moses. It was an adventure each of them would like to have had!

But Moses gave up the luxuries of Pharaoh's household and spent forty years on the backside of the desert. They were profitable years, for there in the loneliness, he came to know God. With this knowledge of God treasured in his heart, he became the leader of his people, and "The man Moses was very great in the land of Egypt." Because of his decision, Moses is remembered better than any other figure of Egyptian history.

YOUR OFFSPRING

Isaiah 30:1-9   Proverbs 22:6

That children are a gift of God, we are frequently told in God's Word. The happiest day in the life of many young couples is when that precious little bundle is brought home from the hospital. But there are many hazards in bringing up children in "the nurture and admonition of the Lord."

"With children we must mix gentleness with firmness," said Charles Haddon Spurgeon. "They must not always have their own way, but they must not always be thwarted. If we never have headaches through rebuking them, we shall have plenty of heartaches when they grow up. Be obeyed at all costs; for if you yield up your authority once, you will hardly get it again."

Among our youth today there is much rebellion and talk of impending revolution. This is not new. This too is covered in God's Word. "Woe to the rebellious children, saith the LORD, that take counsel, but not of me" (Isa 30:1). The trouble with so many children today is they are not willing to "take counsel" from the right One.

"The young lions do lack, and suffer hunger: but they that seek the LORD shall not want any good thing. Come, ye children, hearken unto me: I will teach you the fear of the LORD" (Ps 34:10-11).

THERE'S NO LAW AGAINST IT

1 CORINTHIANS 3:16-23

There are no laws against a lot of things we ought not do, and there are no laws compelling us to do a lot of things we ought to do. This would certainly be an unpleasant world if we relied only upon man-made laws to guide our conduct!

There is no civil ordinance that says we must love our family, try to make others happy, or treat people fairly. We are not threatened with a prison sentence if we are not kind, considerate, forgiving, or helpful. But these attributes should be the by-products of our faith in Jesus Christ. When we fail in these areas, we know we are grieving the Spirit of God who dwells in us.

"What? know ye not that your body is the temple of the Holy Ghost which is in you, which ye have of God, and ye are not your own? For ye are bought with a price: therefore glorify God in your body, and in your spirit, which are God's" (1 Co 6:19-20).

We fail often, and being human will continue to do so, but remembering we have this power dwelling in us, we will have strength provided for obeying the law of Christ.

> Come, Holy Spirit, heav'nly Dove,
> With all thy quick'ning powers;
> Kindle a flame of sacred love
> In these cold hearts of ours.
>
> ISAAC WATTS

SANDS OF THE SEA

MATTHEW 7:24-29

What fun it is to walk along the beach, shoes in hand, bare feet crunching into the damp, cool sand! With shovel and pail, a child can spend hours of delightful play building castles there. But toy houses and mini-castles are the only ones that will stand for any length of time built upon the soft soil.

Lives, like houses, must be built upon a foundation more firm than sand if they are to stand against the onslaughts of the world, the flesh, and the devil. Those who live in hurricane areas know not at what moment a "Camille" or a "Gertrude" may strike, and the ones who survive are usually those who are prepared for such an emergency.

We cannot know at what moment the floods of misfortune, or the winds of worry and weariness, or the rains of reverses may come. So we must build the house of our life upon a rock—the Rock Christ Jesus.

Webster tells us that "sands" may mean "particles of time." Such a foundation for a life is not built in a day but in many days—leaning heavily on His promises and putting complete faith in Him who is "able to keep us from falling."

"Bow down thine ear to me; deliver me speedily: be thou my strong rock, for an house of defence to save me" (Ps 31:2).

BREAKING BREAD TOGETHER

LUKE 24:30-35

In the "good old days" when one spoke of breaking bread together he meant a time of fellowship and hospitality, of friends seated around a table and enjoying a meal together. Our grandmothers, it seems, always had an open door and could set an extra place at the table 'most anytime. Often, whole families could be accommodated overnight or for several days at a time. And Grandma did not consider that she was imposed upon!

In our complicated society, have we lost something valuable by being less hospitable than were our grandparents? There is a warmth in the atmosphere created by congenial friends sitting down and "breaking bread together." Perhaps we should stop in our involved lives and ask ourselves if we should not take time out to invite friends in more often for this kind of Christian fellowship.

Love for our Lord and the souls of men should motivate us to invite in some whom we would like to win for Christ. This provides a wonderful opportunity to share our faith, food, and fellowship.

We read of the disciples coming together to break bread and of Paul's preaching to them. The early church "continued stedfastly in the apostles' doctrine and fellowship, and in breaking of bread, and in prayers" (Ac 2:42).

THINK

In order to stimulate new ideas for his business, many a businessman has placed on his desk the word "THINK." The one thing the modern homemaker doesn't have time for is to stop and think; yet it is something she really needs to take time to do.

The psalmist pronounces that one "blessed" who meditates in the law of the Lord day and night (Ps 1:2). We read that Mary, the mother of Jesus, "kept all these things, and pondered them in her heart" (Lk 2:19). One thing about it, Mother can "ponder" while she is washing dishes, sorting the laundry, or sweeping the kitchen.

A great preacher of another day said, "One pound of beef well chewed and digested and assimilated, will give more strength than tons of beef merely glanced at; and one verse of Scripture chewed and digested and assimilated, will give more strength than whole chapters simply skimmed. Weigh every word you read in the Bible."

"Finally, brethren, whatsoever things are true, whatsoever things are honest, whatsoever things are pure, whatsoever things are lovely, whatsoever things are of good report; if there be any virtue, and if there be any praise, think on these things" (Phil 4:8).

THE POWER OF LOVE

RUTH 1

The story of Ruth is one of those delightful idyls of love which warms our hearts. It is the story of the friendship between two women, and strange as it may seem, it is the love of a girl for her mother-in-law. As the affection of David and Jonathan is the ultimate in the friendship of two men, so is that of Ruth and Naomi for women.

Ruth came into the life of Naomi when she married her son. After the sons had died and Naomi prepared to return to her own land to die, Ruth and Orpah decided to go with her. Orpah changed her mind and returned to her mother's house, while Ruth found her love would not let her be separated from Naomi.

The quietest of women burst into poetry and her words are still repeated as a pledge of devotion.

"Intreat me not to leave thee, or to return from following after thee: for whither thou goest, I will go; and where thou lodgest, I will lodge: thy people shall be my people, and thy God my God: Where thou diest, will I die, and there will I be buried: The LORD do so to me, and more also, if ought but death part thee and me" (Ru 1:16-17).

With these words, the mother-in-law and daughter-in-law relationship ceases to be, and a pair of famous friends walk arm-in-arm down the road of life to an unknown future. Such is the power of love!

LOOK IN THE MIRROR

2 CORINTHIANS 3:6-18

If you want to see yourself as you really are—without benefit of flattering makeup or becoming clothes—look in God's Word. There you can get a good self-portrait. The miracle is that the Holy Spirit, as He applies His Word to our hearts, can transform us into Christ's likeness, and we will hardly recognize ourselves. "But we all, with open face beholding as in a glass the glory of the Lord, are changed into the same image, from glory to glory, even as by the Spirit of the Lord" (2 Co 3:18).

The same metaphor is used in James 1:23, 24 but with a different meaning: "For if any be a hearer of the word, and not a doer, he is like unto a man beholding his natural face in a glass: For he beholdeth himself, and goeth his way, and straightway forgetteth what manner of man he was."

The unsaved one, looking into the Word of God, "beholdeth *himself*" and finds a Mirror that tells it like it is!

Unlike glass mirrors, the Bible not only shows man what is wrong with him, it also tells him what he must do to become a new creation.

NEVER UNDERESTIMATE YOUTH

ECCLESIASTES 11:9-10

Every period of life has its special temptations and dangers. But youth is an especially vulnerable time. It is the forming, fixing period, the spring season of disposition and habit.

To the insurance company, a youth is a bad risk. To the government, he is eligible for the draft at eighteen but until recently was too young to vote. To Mom and Dad he's a tax deduction. Nevertheless, during this time more than any other, the character assumes its permanent qualities, and the young chart their course for time and for eternity.

Youth is capable of marvelous achievement in any realm. Washington was a distinguished colonel when he was twenty-two. Gladstone was a member of Parliament at twenty-two. Shelley was an author at seventeen. Mozart captured Europe with his concertos as early as age four.

What we make of our young people today will determine our world in the future. Mature Christians need to give much time and thought and prayer to our youth. They are a constant challenge, and every effort should be made to win them for Christ, who gave Himself for the sins of every teen-ager.

"Wherewithal shall a young man cleanse his way? by taking heed thereto according to thy word" (Ps 119:9).

GOD'S TEMPLES

PSALM 104:16, 17

On a visit to the Bible lands, one views the majestic cedars of Lebanon with something akin to awe. Then he knows what the poet felt when he said, "the groves were God's first temples." The same feeling comes over one standing amid the giant redwoods of California. In that fragrant sanctuary, the scent of the cones is fresh and pungent. Wandering in silence among the towering trees, one is afraid to speak lest he break the awesome spell.

Standing tall and reaching toward the God who created it, nothing in nature is more majestic than a beautiful tree. Our Christian lives are to be "like a tree planted by the rivers of water" (Ps 1:3).

Dark boughs stretch high toward God, while roots plunged deep in His Word hold us fast. "The righteous shall flourish like the palm tree: he shall grow like a cedar in Lebanon" (Ps 92:12).

Trees also make the child of God remember the Saviour who suffered on Calvary's cross.

> I saw One hanging on a tree,
> In agony and blood;
> He fixed His languid eyes on me,
> As near His cross I stood.
> Oh, can it be, upon a tree
> The Saviour died for me?
> My soul is thrilled,
> My heart is filled,
> To think He died for me!
>
> JOHN NEWTON

HALLOWED BREAD

1 Samuel 21:4-6

Are you teaching your children the Word of God? Is it made a regular part of your family life? Does a scripture verse come quickly to your lips at everyday, common occurrences so that your little ones are served "hallowed bread?"

In the years to come, you will reap great benefits from this kind of daily diet in the home, as will your children when they feed on this kind of food.

Hearts turn always to those places where they have known happiness, felt the warmth of friendliness, and found beauty. Much that our youngsters learn from their school books will be forgotten as life moves on and problems become more complex. But if God's Word is hidden in the heart of a child from his earliest recollection, we are told that "he will not depart from it."

> Thou art the bread of Life,
> O Lord, to me,
> Thy holy Word the truth
> That saveth me;
> Give me to eat and live
> With Thee above;
> Teach me to love Thy truth,
> For Thou art love.
>
> MARY ANN LATHBURY

A DANGEROUS DRUG

JOHN 5:19-24

We sometimes delude ourselves into thinking we can hide from the Lord in church membership or church work. This is like a dangerous drug that puts the soul to sleep. It is not possible to make Christians artificially by confirmation, baptism, sacraments, or rituals. There must be a personal experience with the Saviour before one becomes His child. There must be the realization that salvation is a gift from God which we do not deserve and never could earn.

"As many as received him, to them gave he power to become the sons of God, even to them that believe on his name" (Jn 1:12). We may be trying to make out a good case for ourselves by a respectable life or a correct creed. The way of the world is to rely on self for salvation. God's way points us to Christ. This is the way to peace, to assurance of salvation, to victory, to heaven.

> Come, every soul by sin oppressed,
> There's mercy with the Lord,
> And He will surely give you rest
> By trusting in His word.
> Only trust Him, only trust Him,
> Only trust Him now. He will save you,
> He will save you, He will save you now.
> J. H. STOCKTON

GROWING OLD GRACEFULLY

TITUS 2:2-5

Sooner or later there comes a time of life when what we see by a casual glance in the mirror causes us to stop suddenly and take a longer look. It dawns upon us all at once that we are not as young as we once were. The crow's-feet and wrinkles are sending us a message loud and clear. But length of days are not assured in the Bible for godly living and many of the Lord's devoted people, for one reason or another, depart this life early.

This is not to say that devotion to Jesus Christ and godly living are not owned and blessed of the Lord; they are. Devotion to Jesus Christ and godly living in many instances contribute to physical health and longer life.

What does accrue to the believer is that he is freely justified by grace, and being justified he has peace with God through our Lord Jesus Christ. So we grow old gracefully when we grow old with the grace of God in our hearts. Inner peace will show on our faces and prove to be a better cosmetic than any we buy in a drugstore.

> God keep my heart attuned to laughter
>   When youth is done;
> When all the days are gray days, coming after
>   The warmth, the sun.
> God keep me then from bitterness, from grieving,
>   When life seems cold;
> God keep me always and believing
>   As I grow old.
>
> AUTHOR UNKNOWN

WALK WORTHY

Ephesians 4:1-7

The daily routine tasks and the drudgery that comes with keeping a home, sometimes cause the homemaker to take a dim view of her "calling."

What is this calling? It is described as high, heavenly, holy, and applies not only to duties in the home, but also in a broader sense, to the homemaker's walk through life. It must be high above the level of the world, bearing the stamp of heaven upon it, and holy in the sense that it is separate from all that is sinful and un-Christlike.

We are to walk differently. "That ye henceforth walk not as other Gentiles walk, in the vanity of their mind" (Eph 4:17). Our behavior is not to be patterned after some neighbor whom we choose to be like, but after the precepts in God's Word. We are to walk in love. "And walk in love, as Christ also hath loved us" (Eph 5:2). Our feelings must be sacrificed for the good of others and our lives for the glory of God. We are to walk circumspectly. "See then that ye walk circumspectly, not as fools, but as wise" (Eph 5:15). This means walking with care and caution, looking all around sincerely and consistently to see if danger is coming from any direction.

> Walk in the light!
> So shalt thou know
> That fellowship of love
> His Spirit only can bestow
> Who reigns in light above.
>
> BERNARD BARTON

HUMBLE PIE

ROMANS 12:10-21

The all-time favorite American dessert is said to be apple pie. A slice of warm pie with a wedge of nippy cheese and a good cup of coffee will brighten the dullest day. But there is another kind of pie that is probably the most unfavorite of all and this is "humble pie." None of us like to eat this kind.

It is never easy to go to someone and apologize for some wrongdoing or for a harmful word spoken in haste. Yet when the apology has been accepted in a loving spirit and fellowship has been restored, we feel such a sense of relief that we wonder why we didn't do it sooner. What a better place this world would be if those who love the Lord would seek for understanding and aim at reconciliation. Obedience to the Bible regarding offenses will work in a home as well as in a church.

It requires real Christian character to kindly, courteously, and confidentially straighten out your grievances with others. Some criticisms are imaginary and others are misunderstandings. Eating a little "humble pie" once in a while is good for all of us!

"But I say unto you, That ye resist not evil: but whosoever shall smite thee on thy right cheek, turn to him the other also" (Mt 5:39).

THE THIEF OF TIME

ROMANS 13:11-14

A man named Edward Youngh said, "Procrastination is the thief of time." Does Mr. Procrastination live at your house? It is so much easier to put off cleaning out that closet than it is to get down to the business of doing it.

"I know I ought to write to Aunt Alice—she is old and lonely—but I'll do it tomorrow."

How much good we could do for others if we would follow up our good impulses with immediate action! Procrastination is a deadly enemy which each one of us must conquer, if we are to be in possession of our own lives. There is one area in which you dare not procrastinate, for it is later than you think. "In the day of salvation have I succoured thee: behold, now is the accepted time; behold, now is the day of salvation" (2 Co 6:2).

Have you put off making this most important decision of your life? This is a decision you dare not delay. Accept Jesus Christ as Lord and Saviour *now!*

> Why do you wait, dear brother?
> O why do you tarry so long?
> Your Saviour is waiting to give you
> A place in His sanctified throng.
> Why not? Why not? Why not come to Him now?
>
> GEORGE F. ROOT

GIVE US BREAD

GENESIS 47:12-15

It is said that when Marie Antoinette was told that the people of France were begging for bread, in her ignorance of their real poverty, she cried, "Let them eat cake!"

There are many hungry-hearted people in America today, who are crying for want of spiritual bread while they are being fed pink sodas and chocolate cake.

Spiritual starvation is even more serious than physical undernourishment. "For what shall it profit a man, if he gain the whole world, and lose his own soul?" (Mk 8:36). Poverty programs and Social Security are fine, but what about eternal security?

Although Jesus healed the sick and fed the hungry, He was far more concerned about the spiritual welfare of those to whom He ministered, than He was with their physical well-being.

> Break Thou the bread of life,
> Dear Lord, to me,
> As Thou didst break the loaves
> Beside the sea;
> Beyond the sacred page
> I seek Thee, Lord;
> My spirit pants for Thee,
> O living Word.

> MARY ANN LATHBURY

IN REMEMBRANCE

PSALM 112:1-6

How strange it is that some will go to such great lengths in order to be remembered! Today, in the ancient city of Memphis, once the capital of Egypt, stands a mammoth statue of the publicity-loving Rameses II, whose long and glorious reign lasted sixty-seven years.

Lest the world forget him, he left two colossal statues of himself. One has been removed and now stands majestically before Cairo's main railway station. The other remains at old Memphis but lies prostrate on its back. This ruler of Egypt, who so cruelly oppressed the Hebrews during their Egyptian sojourn, had hundreds of smaller likenesses of himself carved and scattered over Egypt.

The psalmist has a good answer for such vanity. "For in death there is no remembrance of thee: in the grave who shall give thee thanks?" (Ps 6:5).

Our loving Lord would have us remember the price He paid for our redemption. "And he took bread, and gave thanks, and brake it, and gave unto them, saying, This is my body which is given for you: this do in remembrance of me" (Lk 22:19).

If we love Him and remember Him, our name will be written in His book of remembrance.

ON THE SICK LIST

MATTHEW 25:34-40

When was the last time you visited a sick friend or a shut-in? How much better it is to be the one able to do the visiting than to be the one visited! If you yourself are not ill, you should be thankful that it could be your happy privilege to go to see someone who is less fortunate. We can show our gratitude to God for good health by seeking to "bear the infirmities of the weak" (Ro 15:1).

Some are spiritually weak and though they give every indication of enjoying good health, may be sick at heart. What a privilege it is to drop in for a few moments with a word of cheer, a verse from God's Word, and a prayer for their special need. Almost all of us have had times when we would have appreciated greatly a Spirit-filled caller.

> Heavy is the cross they bear,
> But our love that cross can share;
> Dark Thy providence must seem,
> But our cheer can cast a gleam
> On their lot; and in our turn
> Holiest lessons we may learn,
> Where Thine own revealing light
> Streams through pain's mysterious night.
>
> MISS KIMBALL

THAT SPRING OUTFIT

PSALM 45

Isn't it frustrating to open the closet door and find you have nothing "just right" to wear! There are clothes there all right, but something seems to be wrong with everything you examine. So you have one more excuse to go shopping for that spring outfit you've been longing for secretly.

This writer believes that God wants Christian women, living in a modern world, to be as attractive as possible, without sacrificing modesty.

Just as our physical appearance should never be unkempt and tacky, the Bible instructs us in how to "clothe" ourselves so that we are spiritually becoming, also.

"For he put on righteousness as a breastplate, and an helmet of salvation upon his head; and he put on the garments of vengeance for clothing, and was clad with zeal as a cloke" (Is 59:17). "The garments of vengeance" are to be left for God, but we should be sure we are "clad with zeal." "The helmet of salvation" should crown our head.

Nothing is prettier or more feminine than a soft white dress, and nothing is more beautiful than a pure life. "Let thy garments be always white; and let thy head lack no ointment." (Ec 9:8).

I GIVE UP!

Isaiah 40:28-31

Did you ever start to do a job with great enthusiasm, and then when you did not immediately see the expected results, or if the obstacles were greater than anticipated, you became discouraged and were tempted to quit?

"Well, I couldn't do it anyway."

Sometimes the difference between the one who is a failure and the one who is a success, is that one yields to the temptation to quit and the other resists it. This holds especially true in the struggle to live a victorious Christian life. Too often we grow weary in well doing in spite of the fact that we are told, "Let us not be weary in well doing: for in due season we shall reap, if we faint not" (Gal 6:9).

It is so easy for a weary body, a tired mind, and a heavy heart to throw in the towel and give up the struggle with the goal unachieved.

Here is our answer: "Whatsoever is born of God overcometh the world: and this is the victory that overcometh the world, even our faith" (1 Jn 5:4).

ETIQUETTE AND ETHICS

1 CORINTHIANS 13

The great number of etiquette columns in our newspapers and magazines may be an indication of the widespread confusion many people have in the maze of today's social graces. Which fork to use? How to seat the guests at the table? What is proper to wear? Which etiquette expert should you follow?

In the seventeenth century, Louis XIV is said to have searched diligently all over France for a man to teach his grandson the rudiments of proper social behavior. That was a day when a stammered compliment, an awkward bow, or a clumsy finger could ruin a career. The wise man chosen for the task, pointed out to the king that the true foundation of good manners is thoughtfulness of others. What makes one thoughtful? Love.

This is clearly pointed out in Scripture: "Though I speak with the tongues of men and of angels, and have not love, I am become as sounding brass, or a tinkling cymbal" (1 Co 13:1). Later, Paul says, "(Love) doth not behave itself unseemly." Though you may utter the most charming compliments, and though you may stimulate worthwhile conversations around your table, if love is not your basic attitude toward your guests, your excellent manners will appear artificial. And when we are the guest, love will cause our behavior to be what it should be, not "unseemly."

They who would be truly polite are kind with instinctive grace.

OH, THOSE EXAMS!

2 TIMOTHY 2:7-15

The tests our kids have to take at school are almost as hard on us mothers as they are on the kids. During exam time, our offspring, regardless of age, are irritable and fussy; we can't get any work out of them, and everything has to "give" in favor of the exams.

God has testing times for His children, also. These are times when we are given opportunities to prove our knowledge and understanding and faith in Him. Responsibilities and assignments confront us daily, and we find that all of life is a kind of school. A child of God should be diligent and aim for a good grade in managing his opportunities. He is to try hard and earnestly endeavor to be found trustworthy when tested.

We would do well to be prepared for surprise quizzes each day. With God's Word as our textbook, the Holy Spirit as our teacher, and daily conferences with our heavenly Counselor, we will successfully finish the course.

> Should Thy mercy send me
>   Sorrow, toil, and woe;
> Or should pain attend me
>   On my path below;
> Grant that I may never
>   Fail Thy hand to see;
> Grant that I may ever
>   Cast my care on Thee.

JAMES MONTGOMERY

THE BREAD OF MOURNERS

1 Thessalonians 4:13-18

In the Old Testament we read of "the bread of mourners." To the bereaved this is a bread bitter to the taste, unless his faith is resting firmly in the Lord. Sooner or later the sorrow of death reaches into every home. Perhaps if we could get into our minds a clearer picture of the heaven to which our loved ones in Christ have gone, it would help ease the pain of our loss.

The most comforting thought is that one has gone to be with Christ. "So shall we ever be with the Lord" (1 Th 4:17). In writing to the Philippians Paul said, ". . . having a desire to depart, and to be with Christ; *which is far better*" (Phil 1:23).

Realizing that heaven is a place of rest for tired bodies, a place of surcease from sorrow, smooths the loss of the loved one and makes heaven dearer to those who are left behind. "Wherefore comfort one another with these words," Paul said.

While we are eating "the bread of mourners," it is well to remember that for all believers our life is hidden with Christ in God.

> Face to face with Christ, my Saviour,
> Face to face, what will it be?
> When with rapture I behold Him,
> Jesus Christ, who died for me.
>
> MRS. FRANK A. BRECK

BLESS THIS HOUSE

PSALM 127:1-4

The story is told that after President and Mrs. Eisenhower acquired their Gettysburg home, they wrote their pastor in Washington and asked him to come to Gettysburg for a little "house blessing ceremony." When the family had settled in their chairs around the fireplace, the President arose and told how both he and Mrs. Eisenhower had been reared in the presence of an open Bible, revered as the Word of God, and with family prayers as a daily practice. They had lived in many houses during their long association with the army, but this was the first home they could call their very own. So it seemed fitting to dedicate it to God.

What a fine example for young Christian couples who finally find their dream house. Although the payments may extend far into the future, they should lay before God the place where they will rear their children, asking Him to make it a place of health and healing, a haven of tranquility, an abode of love, and a sanctuary of worship.

> The beauty of the house is order;
> The blessing of the house is contentment;
> The glory of the house is hospitality;
> The crown of the house is godliness.
>
> FIREPLACE MOTTO

NO RESPECTER OF PERSONS

ACTS 10:34-35

God is no respecter of persons, nor does He want His children to be. God has no favorites among His children. Financial or social status, race or color matter not to Him. If it were left to us, we would likely cater to the rich and the influential and overlook the poor and the common.

There are many families who spend thousands of dollars to be included in the social register. Most of them do not realize that the highest society on earth is the fellowship of God's "holy people." "Respect of persons" should not be found in the heart of one who has put his faith in the Lord Jesus Christ. We read in Proverbs 24:23, "It is not good to have respect of persons in judgment."

While it is true that our Father makes no distinctions among His children, it is equally true that God honors in a special way those who seek to honor His Son. "If any man serve me, let him follow me; and where I am, there shall also my servant be: if any man serve me, him will my Father honour" (Jn 12:26).

> Come, ye sinners, poor and needy,
> Weak and wounded, sick and sore;
> Jesus ready stands to save you,
> Full of pity, love, and power;
> He is able, He is able,
> He is willing: doubt no more.
>
> JOSEPH HART

A GOOD NEIGHBOR

ROMANS 13:8-10

How heartwarming it is to move into a new home and even while the furniture is still in disarray, have the doorbell ring and a neighbor walk in bearing a still-warm pie—or a salad—or a cake! One is overwhelmed with a sense of being welcomed into the neighborhood. How nice to be able to run next door in a minor emergency and borrow a cup of sugar, or to be borrowed from when the situation is reversed.

But when it comes to "love thy neighbor as thyself," this is quite a different situation! Can it be done? Yes! By the power of the Holy Spirit in the life of the believer. "Love worketh no ill to his neighbour."

Misunderstandings and differences can easily occur in any neighborhood, especially where there are children, but a true believer will seek to settle such in a direct, quiet, forgiving manner.

Do you know your neighbors? Do you ever pray for your neighbors? Do you offer a helping hand in time of need?

"Therefore all things whatsoever ye would that men should do to you, do ye even so to them" (Mt 7:12).

LABOR OF LOVE

PROVERBS 10:6-12

Isn't it strange that something as intangible as love can ease an aching back and rest a tired body? When a sleeping mother must rise from her bed in the wee hours to attend her sick child, love in the mother's heart will lighten that unpleasant task. Many a child's imagined hurt has been healed by a mother's kiss or a pat from her loving hands. Just knowing someone else cares helps in the healing process.

We hesitate sometimes to bring our troubles to God because they must seem so small to Him who sits on the circle of the universe. But if they are big enough to annoy and cause us anxiety, they are big enough to touch His heart of love.

Love is not measured by a merchant's scales. When we administer affection, it is astonishing what magical results we obtain.

> Love divine, all loves excelling,
> Joy of heaven, to earth come down;
> Fix in us thy humble dwelling,
> All thy faithful mercies crown:
> Jesus, thou art all compassion,
> Pure, unbounded love thou art;
> Visit us with thy salvation:
> Enter every trembling heart.
>
> CHARLES WESLEY

SEA OF TRANQUILITY

PSALM 107:21-30

When the telephone rings, the baby begins to cry, the beans are boiling over, and Johnny is in a fight in the backyard, one is likely to long for a smooth sail on a sea of tranquility! These are minor crises in the life of a mother trying to rear her children "in the fear and admonition of the Lord." Weightier anxieties come as they grow older, and Mother fights for them against the world, the flesh, and the devil.

A sea captain explained how navigators now cope with typhoons and monsoons. He said, "When we run into them, we locate the center and then go around it. We narrow the circle until we get into the center where there is a dead calm. There we are safe."

When we are in the center of God's will, He will give us peace and rest in the crises of life; we are safe in Him. There, He keeps our hearts and minds in perfect peace!

> I've anchored my soul in the haven of rest,
> I'll sail the wide seas no more;
> The tempest may sweep o'er the wild stormy deep,
> In Jesus I'm safe evermore.
>
> H. L. GILMOUR

BREAD OF LIFE

JOHN 6:47-51

Certain of the Bible's miracles have particular significance for the homemaker. Since a good portion of her day is taken up with the preparation of meals, she will be more than a little interested in the widow's cruse of oil that never gave out; the multiplying of the loaves of bread by Jesus; the ravens that fed Elijah, etc.

Just as a fresh supply of manna was given to Israel every day, so the Spirit of God breaks anew the bread of life to those who hunger and thirst after righteousness. And as the loaves and fishes in the hands of our Lord were more than enough to feed the famished multitude, so the meat, and milk, and bread, and honey of the Word are more than enough to feed every famished soul.

The amazing fact is that this wonderful bread never grows stale. Generation after generation has been feasting on this bread of life; yet it remains forever fresh. Each reading reveals new gems of truth.

> Lamp of our feet, whereby we trace
> Our path when wont to stray;
> Stream from the fount of heavenly grace,
> Brook by the traveler's way;
> Bread of our souls, whereon we feed,
> True manna from on high;
> Our guide and chart, wherein we read
> Of realms beyond the sky.

BERNARD D. BARTON

THE PLACE OF PRAYER

It is true that "the earth is the LORD'S," and there is no place where prayer may not be heard. A loving God has made it possible for us to pray any time under any circumstance. Yet it is desirable that we have a place of prayer. It was Jesus' habit to withdraw into a solitary place to pray. Matthew tells us, "When he had sent the multitudes away, he went up into a mountain apart to pray: and when the evening was come, he was there alone" (Mt 14:23).

Why is it necessary to have this inner chamber and closed door? Perhaps one reason is that it is not the practice of hypocrites to pray in secret. Prayers to the grandstand require an audience. Skill in phrasing is intended for the ears of men. There is this difference, however: "The LORD seeth not as man seeth; for man looketh on the outward appearance, but the LORD looketh on the heart" (1 Sa 16:7).

Prayer is between the soul and God alone.

> Take time to be holy,
> The world rushes on;
> Spend much time in secret
> With Jesus alone—
> By looking to Jesus,
> Like Him thou shalt be;
> Thy friends in thy conduct
> His likeness shall see.
>
> W. D. LONGSTAFF

FLY YOUR FLAG

NEHEMIAH 8:9, 10

A child once remarked of Principle Rainy that she believed he went to heaven every night, because he was so happy every day. This great saint used a fine metaphor to describe a Christian's joy. "Joy," he said, "is the flag which is flown from the castle of the heart when the King is in residence there."

God does not want His children to be unhappy, and none of us has cause for a constant bad mood. Paul was perhaps the most persecuted of men, yet he was a man of song. Hymns of praise came from his lips in prison and out of prison. Day and night he praised his Saviour.

"Rejoice evermore. Pray without ceasing. In everything give thanks: for this is the will of God in Christ Jesus concerning you" (1 Th 5:16-18). The will of God is not an optional thing. Here we are commanded to do three things: rejoice, pray, give thanks. Reverse the order, and you will wind up with "Rejoice!"

> Rejoice, ye pure in heart,
> Rejoice, give thanks, and sing;
> Your festal banner wave on high,
> The cross of Christ your King.
>
> EDWARD H. PLUMPTRE

THE HOUSEHOLD OF FAITH

GALATIANS 6:6-10

The conscientious wife and mother is very diligent in attending to the needs of her own household, but sometimes she may be a bit negligent about the needs of those who are of the "household of faith." The wise woman "ariseth also while it is yet night, and giveth meat to her household, and a portion to her maidens" (Pr 31:15).

Who are those who are of the household of faith? All who have accepted Jesus Christ as Saviour and Lord!

The laborers are still few for the Lord's harvest. We pray that He "will send forth laborers" but when He calls us to show kindness to a fellow Christian, we are sometimes too busy. If the homemaker waits until she has time, she will never serve the Lord.

It takes more grace to give more and expect less, to work more and shirk less, to commend more and condemn less, to love more and despise less. But it proves to the world that "greater is he that is in you, than he that is in the world" (1 Jn 4:4).

> Give of your best to the Master:
> Give of the strength of your youth;
> Throw your soul's fresh, glowing ardor
> Into the battle for truth.
> Jesus has set the example;
> Dauntless was He, young and brave;
> Give Him your loyal devotion,
> Give Him the best that you have.
>
> HOWARD B. GROSE

THE WEAKER SEX

1 TIMOTHY 2

Woman, made of a man, resulted in the fall into sin and man "made of a woman" resulted in salvation. "But when the fulness of the time was come, God sent forth his Son, made of a woman" (Gal 4:4).

But did you know that there is no incident in Scripture where an individual woman ever acted unkindly toward the Saviour or spoke in a derogatory manner to Him? On the contrary, there are many instances where they pitied Him and other times when they ministered to His needs. "And there followed him a great company of people, and of women, which also bewailed and lamented him" (Lk 23: 27).

Mark tells us that at His crucifixion "There were also women looking on afar off: among whom was Mary Magdalene, and Mary the mother of James the less and of Joses, and Salome; (Who also, when he was in Galilee, followed him, and ministered unto him;) and many other women which came up with him unto Jerusalem" (Mk 15:40, 41).

Today Jesus does not walk the earth in the form of man; however, "the weaker sex" may still find many ways to minister for Him exercising gentleness, compassion, and modesty.

> Many are waiting a kind, loving word,
> Help somebody today!
> Thou hast a message, O let it be heard,
> Help somebody today!
>
> MRS. FRANK A. BRECK

TAKE TIME

PHILIPPIANS 3:12-15

Rome was not built in a day and neither is the Christian life. It should be realized by those who seek to be mature Christians (as we all should!) that this comes, not overnight, but with day-by-day nourishment and exercise in our spiritual lives. God Himself will set the pace, and time each experience to suit His divine purpose for us.

Someone has said, "When God wants to make an oak, He takes an hundred years, but when He wants to make a squash He takes six months." Do you want to be an oak or a squash for the Lord? Our desire, of course, should be to be a strong oak for the Lord, and that as soon as we can! This will require that we make every effort to "know him, and the power of his resurrection, and the fellowship of his sufferings, being made conformable unto his death" (Phil 3:10).

Both the oak and the squash need days of sunshine and days of storm, pain as well as pleasure, failure as well as success, suffering as well as joy, death as well as life. This should not discourage us, but should cause us to look toward eternity.

"Being confident of this very thing, that he which hath begun a good work in you will perform it until the day of Jesus Christ" (Phil 1:6).

ASHES LIKE BREAD

We all have days when we just never should have gotten out of bed. There seem to be a thousand and one small annoyances crowding in on us. This brings to mind the sculptor, who with a chisel in one hand and a mallet in the other, works at shaping a statue. He knows he must use gentle strokes one after another, or he will shatter the whole thing. He works on until the features take shape, and those who enter his studio are charmed and fascinated.

In the process of molding and shaping your Christian life, God sometimes uses strokes of little annoyances and petty vexations. Perhaps the little troubles of life are having more effect upon you than the great ones.

Little annoyances are hewing, digging, shaping, and inter-joining your moral qualities. Use these small irritations to contribute to your spiritual wealth!

Someone has said a bee can suck honey even out of a nettle, and if you have the grace of God in your heart, you can get sweetness out of that which would otherwise irritate and annoy.

> Never be sad or desponding,
> Lean on the arm of thy Lord;
> Dwell in the depths of His mercy,
> Thou shalt receive thy reward.
>
> FANNY J. CROSBY

111

THE GENERATION GAP

Ephesians 6:1-9

There always has been and always will be a gap between parents and their children, because there always has been, in normal circumstances, a gap between the maturity of the parents and that of the children. Then why all the hullabaloo? Have these "gaps" just been discovered?

No matter what the age of the parents or the children, there need not be a "gap" in love and in understanding. If we start early enough, by discipline, prayer, and love, we can work to prevent any gap of understanding.

Much of the rebellion on the part of youth is their attempt to get through to seemingly indifferent parents and find out what is expected of them.

A problem more basic than the generation gap, is what one man refers to as the "*re*generation gap."

Whether he meant the change and renovation of the soul by the spirit and grace of God, is not clear. One thing is clear—if we can get whole families *re*generated, it will solve many problems, and help fill any "gap" between parents and children.

> Lord, speak to me, that I may speak
> In living echoes of thy tone;
> As thou hast sought, so let me seek
> Thy erring children lost and lone.
>
> FRANCES R. HAVERGAL

TEMPER TANTRUMS

Nothing is so exasperating to a mother as to have her child throw a tantrum when corrected for some misdemeanor. It is difficult not to become angry ourselves under such circumstances. But if we do, we put ourselves on the same level with the naughty child. "Brethren, be not children in understanding: howbeit in malice be ye children, but in understanding be men" (1 Co 14:20).

Pity the adult whose bursts of temper have never been checked, and now he is unable to control his actions when he becomes angry.

A violent temper is not only pathetic; to the person who has it, it is unhealthy. One can become so enraged that he does great harm to his own soul. Bitterness takes up residence there, and joy takes its departure. The apostle says, "Laying aside all malice" (1 Pe 2:1). This does not mean to wait until evil things die in our hearts, but there must be a definite act of the will. Some have gone to their graves with a heart full of bitter regrets, because they lashed out in anger at a loved one and then found it was too late to ask forgiveness.

"He that is soon angry dealeth foolishly: and a man of wicked devices is hated" (Pr 14:17).

> Be like Jesus, this my song,
> In the home and in the throng:
> Be like Jesus, all day long!
> I would be like Jesus.
>
> JAMES ROWE

113

WHITE ELEPHANTS

JOHN 14:18-27

Many housewives have searched the house for unwanted items—dust catchers—collected them, and taken them to the P.T.A. or some such organization, to be sold, perhaps for lunch money for underprivileged children. Rare is the household that does not have some "white elephants."

When the kings of Siam wanted to ruin a man in their kingdom, they would present him with a white elephant. The unfortunate man could not get rid of the elephant, for it was sacred and it was a gift from the king. The expense of keeping the useless thing soon impoverished the king's enemy.

The world has many white elephants to offer us, and the child of God is tempted to accept some of these—social prestige, riches, fame. There is nothing wrong with these things per se, but ultimately they can be the downfall of a Christian, perhaps because one begins to trust these things for security and feels no need for God.

"What shall it profit a man, if he shall gain the whole world, and lose his own soul?" (Mk 8:36).

> Take the world, but give me Jesus,
> All its joys are but a name;
> But His love abideth ever,
> Thro' eternal years the same.
>
> FANNY J. CROSBY

FOOLISH QUESTIONS

TITUS 3:1-9

"Why, Mom, why?" How many times we have been impatient with our youngsters because they persisted in asking so many foolish questions! Of course we know that the best way to find out about something is to ask questions.

Jesus, at the age of twelve, was missed by His parents, and "they found him in the temple, sitting in the midst of the doctors, both hearing them, and asking them questions" (Lk 2:46). There are many things in God's Word that He has chosen to keep to Himself. About such, it is wise to "avoid foolish questions." Still, there are vital questions, and we need to go to God's Word to find the answers.

Does my life and conduct adorn the doctrine of God my Saviour? How can I manage my own life until I know what God has planned for me? Do I find myself in God's will, or do I make my own plans, trying to adjust to the constantly changing moral standards of our so-called progressive civilization?

Avoid foolish questions, but "follow righteousness, faith, charity, peace, with them that call on the Lord out of a pure heart" (2 Ti 2:22).

> I am Thine, O Lord, I have heard Thy voice,
> And it told Thy love to me;
> But I long to rise in the arms of faith,
> And be closer drawn to Thee.
>
> FANNY J. CROSBY

ACCENTUATE THE POSITIVE

EPHESIANS 5:19-20

Even though it is foolish, we believe sometimes that if we just won't talk or think about a certain problem, it will go away! On the other hand, if we think and talk and sing about the wonderful things God is doing for us, we are likely to soon come to realize our way is not so filled with hard things after all.

"Talk ye of all his wondrous works" (Ps 105:2).

Someone has said, "The chief pang of most trials is not so much the actual suffering itself as our own spirit of resistance to it." Often the hardships that come to us, are God's way of training us for something He has for us to do. Thank God for the hardships!

Good soldiers are not made by giving them soft jobs. They endure many hardships that are put in their way deliberately, to make them strong. Soldiers of the cross need hard training, too, so Jesus says, "Take up the cross and follow me."

> Sure I must fight, if I would reign;
> Increase my courage, Lord;
> I'll bear the toil, endure the pain,
> Supported by Thy word.
>
> ISAAC WATTS

BREAD AND WINE

Walking into the upper room on Mount Zion in Jerusalem, one is carried back in memory to Jesus' last night on earth. The plain, vaulted room, bare of furniture, at the top of a long stairway, appears to be very old, and one can imagine that the disciples have just left by another door.

Jesus knew that His death was imminent and that the disciples left behind must carry on His work. He must tell them, and somehow they must be given the power to continue the cause for which He soon must die.

So taking common, everyday symbols—bread and wine, the simple food and drink of all Palestine in those days—He immortalized them by likening them to His very body and His blood.

Thus these ordinary provisions were used in an act of worship which has become a Christian sacrament.

"This do in remembrance of Me," He commanded them. He desires that we keep in mind His sacrifice for our sins on the cross.

> I'll live for Him who died for me;
> How happy then my soul shall be!
> I'll live for Him who died for me,
> My Saviour and my God!
>
> RALPH E. HUDSON

WHAT IS HAPPINESS?

PSALM 16

Whether we know it or not, happiness is something we all are seeking. Happiness is a thing you cannot beg or buy or borrow. It cannot be obtained by seeking. Lord Byron lived a life of pleasure and ease, yet he wrote, "The worm, the canker, and grief are mine alone." Jay Gould, the American millionaire, found that happiness is not in money. When dying he said, "I suppose I am the most miserable man on earth."

John Bunyan penned these thoughts on the subject: "The truly happy man was born in the city of regeneration, in the parish of repentance. He owns the largest state in the country of Christian contentment; yet wears the plain garments of humility. He has 'meat to eat that the world knows not of.' He has Gospel submission in his conduct, due order in his affection, sound peace in his conscience, and sanctifying love and joy in his soul."

Happiness is won not by getting, but by giving. It goes out from the heart before it comes in. "A man must contribute to the stock of human joys before he can participate in its profits."

The answer is simple. Happiness is found in Christ alone! "Whoso trusteth in the LORD, happy is he" (Pr 16:20).

> O happy day that fixed my choice
>   On Thee, my Saviour and my God!
> Well may this glowing heart rejoice,
> And tell its raptures all abroad.
>
> PHILIP DODDRIDGE

MAGIC MUSIC

PSALM 149

The Psalms may be called the hymn book of the Bible. How often these verses have brought peace, help, and strength to weary and discouraged Christians! In speaking of the wondrous power of music, Henry Van Dyke said, "It penetrates the bosom and unlocks the doors of secret, dumb, self-consuming anguish, so that the sorrow flowing out may leave the soul unburdened and released. It touches the chord of memory, and the cadence of old songs brings back the happy scenes of the past."

Someone else has observed in another vein, "Many homes are like the frame of a harp that stands without strings. In form and outline they suggest music; but no melody rises from the empty spaces. And thus it happens that home is unattractive, dreary and dull."

Music was an act of worship with Johann Sebastian Bach. The beautiful "Jesu, Joy of Man's Desiring" radiates his love and tenderness, for in it he poured out his soul's devotion to Jesus.

Blessed are those gifted ones who use the ministry of music in the service of the Lord!

There's within my heart a melody
Jesus whispers sweet and low,
Fear not, I am with thee, peace, be still,
In all of life's ebb and flow.
Jesus, Jesus, Jesus—
Sweetest name I know,
Fills my ev'ry longing,
Keeps me singing as I go.

L. B. BRIDGERS

GOD'S GUIDANCE

Isaiah 58:9-11

It is easy these days to soon come to the end of our own wisdom. Many decisions must be made daily. We are assured over and over in the Bible that God is willing to guide us.

Solomon, the wisest of men, said, "In all thy ways acknowledge him, and he shall direct thy paths" (Pr 3:6). Never will He guide in any way that is contrary to His Word. We must read it carefully each day with a prayer that God will speak to us from its pages. "Thy word is a lamp unto my feet, and a light unto my path" (Ps 119:105).

The Holy Spirit indwelling us will guide us. "As many as are led by the Spirit of God, they are the sons of God" (Ro 8:14). The habit of daily seeking God's guidance should be cultivated. We should seek it with sincerity and an open mind. Once His will is known it should be followed, regardless of the cost.

Often He will lead only one step at a time. After we take one step in faith He will reveal the next. "I will instruct thee and teach thee in the way which thou shalt go: I will guide thee with mine eye" (Ps 32:8).

> Guide me, O Thou great Jehovah,
> Pilgrim thro' this barren land;
> I am weak, but Thou art mighty,
> Hold me with Thy pow'rful hand.
> WILLIAM WILLIAMS

UNFAILING FAITH

For any who would serve the Lord, faith is a basic requirement. "Without faith it is impossible to please him" (v. 6).

Someone has said, "Faith is abandonment to Jesus." Abandonment denotes complete surrender to the mercy of someone else. It clings to nothing but Christ even to the extent of crying, "Though He slay me, yet will I trust in him" (Job 13:15). Such faith is the result of knowledge of God and His Word. "Faith cometh by hearing, and hearing by the word of God" (Ro 10:17).

Peter urges us to add to our faith virtue, knowledge, temperance, patience, godliness, brotherly kindness and love; and if you do, he tells us, "ye shall neither be barren nor unfruitful in the knowledge of our Lord Jesus Christ" (2 Pe 1:5-8).

A Christian writer noted this: "Prayer is the faith that asks; thanksgiving is the faith that takes." Sometimes we should stop asking and accept what God has for us.

Believe that ye have received, and ye shall have (Mk 11:24, par).

> Encamped along the hills of light,
> Ye Christian soldiers, rise,
> And press the battle ere the night
> Shall veil the glowing skies.
> Against the foe in vales below
> Let all our strength be hurled;
> Faith is the victory, we know,
> That overcomes the world.
>
> JOHN H. YATES

121

GIVEN TO HOSPITALITY

ROMANS 12:9-13

Is being hospitable worth the price? Is anything worth the effort it takes, when it has to be squeezed in between chauffeuring Jane to music lessons and Johnny to Scouts, studying for a Sunday school lesson, cooking the roast, bathing the baby, et cetera, et cetera, et cetera?

Many will remember with nostalgia those happy times when as children we were told, "The preacher is coming to dinner"; or some missionary, or servant of Christ was to be a guest in the home for a few days. The stories and exciting adventures in foreign lands that were related around the dinner table will never be forgotten. Accounts of miracles performed by the Lord in faraway places, have had a wonderful influence on the lives of many in homes where such hospitality abounded.

Boys and girls in such homes have often given their lives in full-time service for the Lord as a result of such contacts with these saints. Personal contact with soldiers of the cross enriches the lives of the young folks in the home (as well as the adults!) in a way they are never able to forget.

Yes, it is worth the effort, even if we have to leave something else undone!

"Use hospitality one to another without grudging" (1 Pe 4:9).

BREAD AND STONES

It is not likely that anyone reading these lines would, if her son asked for bread, give him a stone. Yet many of us are not giving our children spiritual bread, whether or not they ask for it.

Most parents are keenly aware of their duties and responsibilities to their children. When parents teach their children the commandments and judgments of the Lord, it will be likened unto them "as the days of heaven upon the earth" (Deu 11:21).

The first Bible training a child receives should be in the home. These times should be joyful and happy, and parents will be rewarded by watching the spiritual development of their children.

Children should be taught in the home the importance of confessing sins to God so prayer will be answered. A Christian home with a daily family altar is good insurance against juvenile delinquency. We must double our efforts to counteract the effect of the mad pace of today's world on our children and ourselves. The world will give them many "stones." Let's feed them on the bread of God's Word.

"Thy word is a lamp unto my feet, and a light unto my path" (Ps 119:105).

> How firm a foundation, ye saints of the Lord,
> Is laid for your faith in His excellent word!
> What more can He say, than to you He hath said,
> To you who for refuge to Jesus have fled?
>
> GEORGE KEITH

ANXIOUS CARE

PHILLIPIANS 4:6-7

"Be careful for *nothing!*" Do you believe it? "Nothing" means *nothing* and everything means everything. It's as simple as that. No anxiety ought to be found in the believer. To doubt God is to believe that He is not all-powerful.

Our afflictions, trials, and difficulties may be great and varied, but if God is taken at His word, all worry and anxious care will disappear from the life of one of His own. Whether we realize it or not, there must be something in our subconscious which tells us that we can work our way out of our difficulties and that if we mull over our anxieties and harbor them in our thoughts, we will somehow be able to alleviate them.

How foolish! God has given us here the formula for peace in our hearts, and so often we refuse to accept it. We are afraid to trust Him completely with our problems.

Why not put your faith to the test and "with thanksgiving let your requests be made known unto God?" The peace of God that will flood your heart will be that "which passeth all understanding."

> Be not dismayed, whate'er betide,
> God will take care of you;
> Beneath His wings of love abide,
> God will take care of you.
>   C. D. MARTIN

TENSION AND HYPERTENSION

ROMANS 8:26-27

You know how your sewing machine acts when there is too much tension. The thread tangles or breaks, and you find yourself in trouble trying to untangle the threads. Just so we need to learn to live with less tension. We cannot violate constantly the laws of nature by not getting enough rest, by overeating, and in other ways, without sooner or later paying the price.

God made natural laws as He did spiritual laws, and one can cut off his service to the Lord by disobedience to either of these types of laws.

On the other hand, we need *some* tension. A musician will give a much better performance if he is "keyed up." Without tension, what would make your watch run? Not to mention the many push-buttons we enjoy to help us carry on our household tasks!

So we need an upward tug to pull us toward self-improvement and toward spiritual growth, if we are to arrive at healthy, spiritual living.

> Just when I need Him, Jesus is strong,
> Bearing my burdens all the day long;
> For all my sorrow giving a song
> Just when I need Him most.
>
> WILLIAM POOLE

FAITH AND FASHION

COLOSSIANS 2:6-8

One's appearance is said to be an expression of his personality. If that is so, the fact that one is a child of God should be evident in his appearance. It is hardly possible to dress in some of the far out fashions of the day and at the same time glorify the Lord Jesus. This is not to say that a believer should be slovenly in his appearance, as though he were saying to the world, "It does not matter what I wear or how I look." Too often this attitude is a cover-up for laziness and lack of self-respect or respect for others.

In line with the moral climate of our times, today's fashions are leaning more and more toward the "unisex" styles. The Christian will find guidelines in God's Word concerning this, such as, "The woman shall not wear that which pertaineth unto a man, neither shall a man put on a woman's garment: for all that do so are an abomination unto the Lord thy God" (Deu 22:5).

Satan delights to break down moral standards by using clothing styles or any other effective tool. To use good taste and dress attractively and modestly is a part of our Christian testimony. If we are to represent Him on earth our appearance should be worthy of Him.

A TREATISE ON THE TONGUE

JAMES 3:3-13

Did you ever realize, as soon as you said something, that you had said the wrong thing? James' epistle has given us quite a discourse on the tongue, that "little member." We seem to have no difficulty in controlling a "big member," an arm, a hand, or a foot, but when it comes to that "little member" it is a different story! This "unruly evil, full of deadly poison" is allowed to run wild, to take its own course and wreak havoc.

There are few who have the ability to consistently say the right thing, in the right way, and at the right time. When you open your mouth you "put your foot into it," and all efforts to correct the mistake turn out to be greater disasters than the original error. This is an old, old problem.

TV performers rely on "idiot cards" to prompt them. Shakespeare's *Hamlet* says, "We must speak by the card, or equivocation will undo us."

The Christian has a wonderful prompter and guide for his speech in the Word of God. When the loving Lord reigns in the heart He will control the "unruly member," and gracious words will proceed out of the mouth.

"If any man among you seem to be religious, and bridleth not his tongue, but deceiveth his own heart, this man's religion is vain" (Ja 1:26).

THE LIVING BREAD

JOHN 6:51-58

Bread is an important word. It means life to the hungry, and is ultimately that for which they put in forty hours of work a week. It is equally necessary to the day laborer and to the financier. Bread is so great a thing and yet so simple, that God chose it as a symbol of His blessed Son, the Living Bread.

But if bread is not eaten, it cannot give nourishment to the body and sustain life. So it is, that even though the Living Bread was offered up for our sins on the cross; if we do not assimilate and partake of this Bread, He cannot give us eternal life.

"He that eateth of this bread shall live for ever" (v. 58). Have you partaken of the Bread of Life?

> Softly and tenderly Jesus is calling,
> Calling for you and for me,
> See on the portals He's waiting and watching,
> Watching for you and for me.
> Oh! for the wonderful love He has promised,
> Promised for you and for me;
> Tho' we have sinn'd, He has mercy and pardon,
> Pardon for you and for me.
>
> WILL L. THOMPSON